NEIL SIMON'S

Lost in
YONKERS

NEIL SIMON'S

Lost in YONKERS

THE ILLUSTRATED SCREENPLAY OF THE FILM

NEIL SIMON

Foreword by
RAY STARK

Introduction by
MARTHA COOLIDGE

Photographs by
ZADE ROSENTHAL
and other contributors

Edited by
ANNE HOY

A NEWMARKET PRESS PICTORIAL MOVIEBOOK
NEWMARKET PRESS • NEW YORK

93 94 95 96   10 9 8 7 6 5 4 3 2 1

Library of Congress Cataloging-in-Publication Data

Simon, Neil.
    [Lost in Yonkers]
    Neil Simon's lost in Yonkers : the illustrated screenplay / Neil
Simon ; introduction by Martha Coolidge ; foreword by Ray Stark. —
1st ed.
        p. cm.
    Companion book to the motion picture, Lost in Yonkers.
    ISBN 1-55704-171-7
    1. Lost in Yonkers (Motion picture)   I. Coolidge, Martha.
II. Title.
PN1997.L7453S56 1993
791.43'72—dc20   93-7848
                                            CIP

Quantity Purchases
Companies, professional groups, clubs, and other organizations may qualify for special terms when ordering quantities of this title. For information, write Special Sales, Newmarket Press, 18 East 48th Street, New York, NY 10017, or call (212) 832-3575.

Produced by Newmarket Productions, a division of Newmarket Publishing & Communications Company: Esther Margolis, director, Keith Hollaman, editor, Joe Gannon, production manager.

Book Design by Eric Baker Design Associates, Inc.

Manufactured in the United States of America

First Edition

OTHER NEWMARKET PICTORIAL MOVIEBOOKS INCLUDE:

Dances with Wolves: The Illustrated Story of the Epic Film
Far and Away: The Illustrated Story of a Journey from Ireland to America in the 1890s
The Inner Circle: An Inside View of Soviet Life Under Stalin
City of Joy: The Illustrated Story of the Film
Gandhi: A Pictorial Biography

CONTENTS

PRODUCER'S FOREWORD ON NEIL SIMON'S *LOST IN YONKERS*

RAY STARK

More and more Neil Simon is approaching writing for the theater and screen as did Graham Greene with his wonderful novels—that is, Neil writes plays and films that are entertainments as well as those that examine life on a much more ambitious level.

Lost in Yonkers is very much a comedy, but a human comedy that observes life through the prism of a family that is barely functioning. They are a gallery of walking wounded, seen through the eyes of two youngsters who are wise enough to separate themselves psychologically from the group while retaining sympathy for them.

While the individuals are very strongly drawn, my feeling is that the real story lies in the larger view of how pain, human differences and lots of humor go into the making of a family. And how one adjusts to this environment. It's a timeless theme and Neil pursued it with great dramatic insight to win a Pulitzer Prize.

Having a long relationship with Neil—this is our eleventh film together—I wanted very much to bring this play to the screen. What I didn't want to do was make it as a museum piece or a filmed play: I wanted it to be a movie that moved like a movie, but also one that captured the humanity of Neil's story. Neil was even more in favor of this approach and saw the screenplay as a way to extend his thoughts and characters.

He and director Martha Coolidge have created a film that realizes so much of our hopes—one that may suggest a city in its title, but is universal in its view of life.

Author Neil Simon on location for
Lost in Yonkers.

TALKING WITH NEIL SIMON

The only living playwright with a theater named after him, the author of twenty-seven plays (to date) and screenwriter of ten of their film adaptations, the most commercially successful playwright in history, Neil Simon is also, according to *Newsweek*, "the legendary nice guy of the American theater." As the filming of his screenplay of *Lost in Yonkers* took place, the author talked about that process, the creative process and other matters, both serious and lighthearted, on location in the Cincinnati area and on the movie sets in Los Angeles.

Where did the idea come from, to create this family?

"*Lost in Yonkers* is not about the families I've written about before. It's not, like the Brighton Beach trilogy, about a part of my life. This is about a dysfunctional family, but in a time warp, because there were no dysfunctional families in the thirties or forties or fifties—they were just called crazy people. So they were the kinds of people I had met and knew. What interested me is, what made them dysfunctional? Does it just happen genetically? What about the circumstances of the grandmother's life?

"I don't write social and political plays, because I've always thought the family was the microcosm of what goes on in the world. I write about the small wars that eventually become the big wars.

"Grandma was literally twisted in childhood—she was caught in a riot and her foot was crushed. She comes to this country, loses her husband, loses her first two children. She teaches the four remaining children to survive at any cost, and that's what they do. Except Bella. Bella has this incredible tenacity, strength, humor. She may be a person who I would call emotionally arrested for want of a more clinical term, but she's one of the strongest characters I've ever written. She eventually stands up to her mother; she's very loving and very giving. She's going to be all right.

"There's a moment in the play with her nephews, when the older brother, who's about fifteen, says to the younger brother, 'Did you ever notice that everyone on Pop's side of the family is crazy? Mom always used to tell me that.' That used to get a roar from the audience, because there isn't a family that doesn't say it. Pop says Mom's side of the family is crazy, Mom says it's the other side.

"Half of this piece is a comedy, really, a big-laughs comedy—which is the way I seem to write. Because I'm always trying to find the human comedy. There is laughter here, and the boys provide it, because they're a sort of Greek chorus, on the outside looking at this, and saying, 'Wow, what a crazy family.' And they're terrified because it's very Dickensian being left in the hands of people who can't cope well with life.

"This is one of the dilemmas, the conflicts in the piece. In *Broadway Bound*, the older brother Stan keeps asking Eugene for the essential ingredient in comedy, and when Eugene can't answer, Stan says, 'Conflict!' When he asks for the other key ingredient, and Eugene can only come up with, 'More conflict?' Stan says, 'The key word is *wants*. In every comedy, even drama, somebody has to want something and want it bad. When somebody tries to stop him—that's conflict.' To me, setting people in conflict with each other is like what those Chinese jugglers do, spinning one plate, then another, then another. I wanted to keep as many plates spinning as I could."

Some people feel that the production designer, the performers and others have found a sense of Hansel and Gretel in this story.

"I know what they mean. When you speak to other people when you're doing a project—the actors, the director, the producer—they always have a different take on what the author means, which is very good, because they can always enhance it. There is Hansel and Gretel, because these two kids are left alone in the forest by the father, and the mean witch is the grandmother. And some of the other people are scary, and there's one big rabbit who is going to help them: Bella."

They go into the candy store like the gingerbread house.

"It's interesting. . . I remarried six years ago and adopted my wife's child, so now I have an eight-year-old child, and I also have a thirty-five-year-old daughter and a twenty-nine-year-old daughter, both of whom have children. And living with this eight-year-old child and reading her books at night, I was in the world of Hansel and Gretel, in a fairy-tale world. I see how much she loves that. How the mind works is very mysterious.

"I'm a crossword puzzle fanatic, and you'll always see the clue 'fairy-tale figure' and the answer is always 'ogre.' So you can't do without an ogre in the puzzle, and you can't do a regular film without some sort of villain."

You have lived with this as a play—how was it to turn it into a movie?

"This is one of the times I really liked the process. With Martha Coolidge, the avenues of expression were open between both of us, no traffic in between.

"Generally in doing a screenplay I get a second chance to fix the things that I didn't think worked, and I also get some of the offstage characters of the play into the film. At least one character becomes major in this film, who is Johnny, the only boyfriend Bella has ever been able to relate to. He has more chronic problems than she does, but they fall in love with each other.

"In the play, we used voice-overs of the father's letters to the boys while the scenery was changed in the dark. Now we show him on the road, on a boat, on a train filled with soldiers. We get to see what's going on in America during the war, and also the connection the father still has for his sons, hoping to get back and release them from the dungeon he left them in."

How does the film differ from the play?

"The thing that Martha Coolidge made most important to everybody—especially Mercedes Ruehl and Irene Worth, who had done the play before—was, 'We are no longer doing a play, film is very different, it doesn't have to be as big. You can do a gesture with your eyes, you can just look at somebody, you don't have to say a big speech.' I cut tons and tons of big speeches out—I think it is truly a film now. I just used the play *Lost in Yonkers* as source material."

You've written this as a play, and again as a screenplay—what was the creative process like?

"Well, the creative process amazes me right up to the moment I see a piece with an audience. I know the subject very well, but how I got to each thing and how it worked out toward the end where everything fits right amazes me. I always feel that there is some other brain, maybe a subconscious brain, that does that work. I'm only dealing with the conscious brain, who thinks—yes—I'm writing this, you have a character come in and do this. But the other brain back there is saying no, no, no, put something like this in and you'll use it later. It's called the muse, it comes from someplace else. You always feel you're a middle man, the typist or the secretary. It mystifies me, and yet I do think I always know what I'm doing.

"I'm instinctive—which is a dangerous way of writing. It's like going into a forest with a hunting knife but no compass. You just use your own intuition to get yourself out on the other side. And that's what happens—I write a scene and say, I know I'll get out of it the right way. What I care about is, is it really important, is it really relevant? Is it going to hold the

Neil Simon and director Martha Coolidge during the filming of *Lost in Yonkers*.

audience, is it going to move the piece along? Is it funny, is it exciting? I want that scene to work. The next scene will take care of itself, and they usually do.

"So, it's a process. I don't know how it works. I know I'm going to write a book in about a year or so, a theatrical memoir about all the plays and films I've written—not just the productions of them, but what the process was. I'm hoping maybe I will discover how I've done it, because I don't know.

"I read the newspapers, I read the critics to find out what the themes of my plays are. I haven't the slightest idea. Nor, I think, should an author know what the themes of his plays are, because he'll start to write predictably. It's what I learned from the one play-writing book I ever read—by John van Druten—who said, don't plan everything out, it takes the fun out of the writing, it becomes just work. The other thing is, if you know what the ending is, the audience will see that you know, so they'll all guess it. I never know, I just keep writing."

When you were creating Lost in Yonkers, *what surprised you in the process?*

"The dynamics of it. I knew that Bella, for example, was going to call the family together to try to tell them she wanted to borrow five thousand dollars to open a restaurant with this man who she's reluctant to say is retarded—he works as an usher in a movie theater, he's forty years old—and she knows that it's going to be difficult telling them. And so I write the scene, and as I'm writing it, I realize it's very funny, in a poignant way. It's very funny, because how do you tell this information? She sits down, she gets the family all together, and then she says, 'Okay, who wants to start?' And it goes on, and she's pushed by Louie, 'What do you mean, what does this guy want?' And finally she yells out, 'He doesn't want my money, he wants something more important.'

"Louie says, 'What could be more important than that?' She says, 'Me, he wants me. I want to be his wife, I want to have his babies.'

"And I see the audience just stop. It just stops. I didn't know I was going to write that, I didn't know that it was going to become very poignant, to the point that I would cry myself when I saw Mercedes do it in the beginning. Because this is such a cry of 'let me be my own person,' which is a cry, I think, of most people in the world who are to some degree held down."

Have you ever tried to figure out what it is that makes you see comedy in such painful situations?

"Well, I know that comedy based on comic situations has no weight to it. You can laugh at it, but you forget it the minute you're out of there. It's not hard to make people laugh. Comics stand up and tell one joke after another and I'll laugh. But what I like to write is comedy as though it's drama. The underpinnings have to be very strong, the stakes have to be very important for all of the characters, and if you took out all the humor, it would still hold together as a story.

"When I started writing plays I was warned by people like Lillian Hellman, 'You do not mix comedy with drama.' But my theory was, if it's mixed in life, why can't you do it in a play?

"I don't look to inject humor into a piece. I just find it in the characters. There has to be some point of view that's humorous, or it's the rhythms of their speech, or their take on the world—whether it's as offbeat as Bella or as observant as the boys.

"I only know what some aspects of my humor are, one of which involves being completely literal. And saying something that's instantly identifiable to everybody. People come up to you after the show and say, 'I've always thought that, but I never knew anyone else thought it.' It's a shared secret between you and the audience.

"There are various styles and attitudes toward comedy. When I worked on *Your Show of Shows*, Larry Gelbart was the wittiest, cleverest man I'd ever met, Mel Brooks the most outrageous. I never knew what I was. I still don't know. Maybe I had the best sense of construction of the group.

"What I write is the 'well-made play'—a play that tells you what the problem is, then shows you how it affects everybody, then resolves it.

Resolution doesn't mean a happy ending—sometimes I have hopeful endings, sometimes optimistic ones. I try never to end the play with two people in each other's arms—unless it's a musical. A play should never really come to an end. The audience should leave saying, 'What's going to happen to them now?'"

Do you find that your writing has moved away from jokes and more to humor?

"I do want to be taken more seriously, yet I want to hear the laughter in the theater. The laughs are very often the same gratification to the audience as letting themselves cry. They're interchangeable emotions.

"The Brighton Beach trilogy, *Jake's Women* and *Lost in Yonkers* are basically dramas that have a great deal of comedy in them. I hate the word 'jokes,' I hate the word 'one-liners' pertaining to the things I write. Sometimes I do have one-liners, but as Walter Kerr, the critic for the *New York Times*, once said, 'to be or not to be' is a one-liner. You become very succinct, you wrap up a thought in one specific line, and it could be a very wise line and no one would say anything. But if it happens to be funny, it's called a one-liner."

What do you consider your strongest suit as a writer? What's your weakest suit?

"I think my blue suit is my weakest."

I knew it would come to this.

Glittering prizes for the play *Lost in Yonkers*, as seen in this ad. The Broadway hit also won four Drama Desk Awards, including Best Play; three Outer Critics Circle Awards, again including Best Play; plus the Clarence Derwent Award, while Neil Simon garnered the Drama League Award.

This text includes quotations from "Neil Simon: The Art of Theater X," based on interviews with the author by James Lipton, in Vol. 125 of *The Paris Review*, Winter 1992. We are grateful to *The Paris Review* for permission to include these excerpts here.

ON DIRECTING *LOST IN YONKERS*

MARTHA COOLIDGE

What resonated for me in Neil Simon's *Lost in Yonkers* was the quality and appeal of the writing, the development of the characters and the seriousness of the conflicts involved. There are few staggeringly great writers around, but here was an opportunity to work with one. It all starts with the material. At our first meeting, Neil and I had a meeting of the minds about what this material was, and that I was the right person to do it.

The story in *Lost in Yonkers* is primal, with the power of fairy tales. Beyond the specifics of Yonkers in 1942, a place and date that anchor the Kurnitz family in rock-hard reality, there is something in this story that affects everyone. I saw the play as a tourist and saw how the audience identified with it. I read Neil's adaptation of it for the film and realized that when the boys first come down the street to Grandma's candy store, which is all locked up but beckons tauntingly to them, forbidding them to touch but letting them look, we are seeing Hansel and Gretel. Their Aunt Bella, the youngest of Grandma's children, kept at home and childlike, the better to wait on her crippled mother: who is she but Cinderella? Bella, Bella, Cinderella.

These two stories are intertwined—of Jay and Arty and their coming of age in the gingerbread house, and Bella, the person in all of us who has been emotionally denied and seeks her freedom and Prince Charming. Grandma is not only a stern German-Jewish immigrant but the wicked old witch and the ugly stepmother. This family shares a universal truth with all families. The fairy-tale basis of this story exists in every culture.

The ageless classicism of these characters and their situation takes *Yonkers* out of the period-piece class. To me, it's a story about a miracle. That there are people in the world who have love to give and the courage to go out and give it when it is nowhere around them. That Bella and the boys and even their petty gangster Uncle Louie can find it in the face of the denying atmosphere that Grandma has created is a metaphor for what life is all about.

This story resonated for me for other reasons too. It shares some of the themes of my earlier work. My entertainment features, like *Rambling Rose, Crazy in Love, Real Genius,* and *Valley Girl,* and my documentaries, serious dramatic pieces like *Not a Pretty Picture,* an autobiographical story of date rape, are all about personal choices, personal heroism and survival on some kind of moral level. *Lost in Yonkers* asks, how do we survive

Producer Ray Stark and director Martha Coolidge are rarely at a loss for words.

cruelty and deprivation to live full lives, and how do we learn the miraculous lessons and make the choices that enable us to do that?

Of course *Lost in Yonkers* is also funny. It's not *Medea*. Comedy makes us laugh, I think, because there is a sudden new discovery or revelation of a truth that has some pain in it, and that's why it's funny. Comedy is based on pain and truth, and if the comedy is more than a skit, there is always dramatic conflict in it.

We didn't play it on a metaphoric level: you cannot play a symbol because these people are utterly real. The mythic basis for them is subliminal. But recognizing the metaphor in the piece helped me determine the design of the picture. David Chapman's production design sets the mood and defines the environment and underscores the themes of the movie. It recalls a prison camp picture: the boys even break out, escape by a tunnel at one point, and Uncle Louie tells a story of Grandma locking her children in the closet. So I specifically made the candy store a kind of entryway—it

Brad Stoll and Mike Damus, who play Jay and Arty, with Martha Coolidge on Grandma's back porch.

tantalizes you with all that beautiful candy (a little more than you might have had in 1942 in the middle of the war), and its big windows look onto the world and the busy life out there.

Upstairs, on the other hand, Grandma's apartment, her inner sanctum, is like a prison, with little windows, dark, suffocating, and almost dead, except for the little touches that Bella and the boys have brought in.

In making documentaries, I learned how ideas or struggles are expressed through objects and environments, and so I fought hard to shoot *Yonkers* in a real city, not on a lot. No matter how good that lot set is, the turn in the road lasts only a half a block, and it always looks a little bit like Disneyland. I felt that every ounce of reality that came through that camera lens—because the camera can *only* photograph reality—would add to the truthful feeling of our Yonkers and make it as real as it could be. Those old cars drive by on real-size streets, not seven-eighths-size versions, and when you look down any street, it goes on forever.

The emotional depth in this piece is so strong that if it weren't visually deep it would feel like a play—shallow, as if they had built paper walls. Because the metaphors are so strong, because the film comes from a play, I felt it was essential to bring reality into it.

The movie is different from the play because we get to see the difference between Grandma's house and the rest of the world. That world is normal and colorful and has people and movies and flirting and all kinds of things going on in it. Because we can go outside with Bella, the boys and Louie, Grandma's Venus Flytrap never gets too oppressive. When you are inside the apartment or store, you see or hear what's outside. We can compare these worlds at all times.

The new characters that Neil introduced in the screenplay also opened up the piece and altered it. In the play we only hear about Bella's beau, the movie-theater usher Johnny, and Hollywood Harry and his brother, the gangsters chasing Louie. The chase adds a fun movie-like element to the picture, and all three men are extensions of the characters' movie fantasies into their lives.

Johnny—a wonderfully poetic, touching figure—especially enriches Bella's character. On Broadway we only saw her in relation to the boys and Grandma, and very little with her brother Louie. But she changes when

she is with Johnny; she becomes more womanly and adult, more self-suffi-
cient, more like us. And we see that she is much better off than he is. He
really is retarded.

Bella is handicapped, but more emotionally than intellectually. She
has been handicapped by the label put on her by her family and the period: today we would say she had a learning disability. She's not retarded or
crazy but emotionally arrested. She is a woman who has never been
allowed to grow up, a child-woman. But she has a gift that has helped her
through circumstances many other people could not survive. She has an
amazing and unique ability to love, to give from a wellspring of emotion,
despite the repressive environment of her childhood, which still surrounds
her. Her transformation, which we will see, was always written into her
character, but the movie gives us more opportunities to show it.

In the play, frozen inside the proscenium arch, Bella cannot leave,
but to show that power is changing hands in the family, Neil had her turn
music on the radio. Grandma lets her, but Neil was uncomfortable with
that because Grandma would never change so much. In the film, Bella
actually walks out. Her character is much more together; she grows up.

You enter Yonkers through the point of view of the boys—their reactions tell you the story, and they comment on it, with the innocent
pragmatism of wise children. They are the source of much of the humor of
the piece. Movies are subjective, and you always look through certain characters' eyes or in a certain way. Here the boys' responses are very
important, and they, especially the oldest boy, Jay, grow up during the picture. You know that this experience changed their lives forever.

I cast the boys much younger than they were in the play, because I
felt their experience living with Grandma mattered more if they could really be hurt. On stage, an adult played a teenaged Jay whose voice had
changed. How is Grandma or even Louie going to push him around? It's
less likely. These boys are small enough to be genuinely terrorized. They
are the spine of the picture.

But Bella is the flower and she blossoms in the film. She is the light
side of the family, and Grandma is the dark. While Bella is flamboyant,
Grandma is contained. In cutting, we would continually remind ourselves to
keep her in, among all the hyperactive characters, and show her reactions
and feelings.

Grandma is a woman with very little imagination, a refugee in a generation of people who came to this country in grief and poverty. She lost her father in Germany and her husband, and the first two of her six children died here as she was struggling alone to make a living. She never could overcome the loss and the guilt of outliving these family members, who she perhaps loved more than the others, and because of this she shut down. She fed and clothed the four children who survived—Bella and Louie, the boys' father, Eddie, and Gert, whom we meet later in the piece—but she denied them the very thing they needed, which was nurturing.

Grandma came from a generation of very tough-minded people. They coped with the first world war, the Depression and the second war. They were not introspective, self-searching people in those days; they were not concerned with supporting the self-esteem of others. She reminded me of my own grandmother, who was a very scary woman to me when I was a young girl. When I was about eight years old, my father was dying of cancer—he was forty—and I was brought with my brother and sister to stay

Mercedes Ruehl and Susan Merson rehearse as Bella and Gert in the after-dinner scene, while Martha Coolidge (right) **looks on. Brad Stoll, Richard Dreyfuss and Irene Worth wait for their cues.**

Mercedes Ruehl (left) and Irene Worth take a break with director Martha Coolidge just before playing the start of their final scene. "I think women are generally more analytical in psychological terms than men are," says Ruehl. "Men deal with events and say event A led to event B and the synthesis of event A and event B is event C. It's more linear thinking. While women say, why do you think she behaved this way all her life? Why do you think Grandma is so withholding and cold now? "

with my grandmother while my parents went on their last trip together. I knew something terrible was happening. My grandmother took on an enormous, frightening character. She ran the house with great discipline, and washed my sister's mouth out with soap for saying something. Her son—my father—was dying. Six people close to her died in a period of several years. I made *An Old-Fashioned Woman* about her, and she says this in the movie, "time and keeping busy cure everything." She was quite withholding and yet I knew she loved me. And I loved her.

Survival vs. emotion and love were always issues for me, and they focused in *Lost in Yonkers*. I do not think you can do good work unless you have deep personal themes. Even though a director does not write a piece, I believe that you pick material because its themes, overt and subterranean, click with your own. You work out of yourself; it is the only way you can work. So I jokingly call myself a method director.

Grandma changes more in the film than she does in the play. I agree with Neil that she cannot change for Bella, that she is locked into a rigid

relation with her. But the boys are a whole new force in the family, and by battling with her through the whole movie, making her take the gift of their picture as they leave at the end, by loving her in their own way, by forcing her to become a grandmother, she is made to realize she is loved. She has never really experienced that. We leave the interpretation open, for each viewer to make, but I think she sees that she is going to have visits from them, they are going to phone her, and call her on her rough stuff, and make her be a grandmother. It's not going to be an especially warm relation, but there is a place in their lives for her, and a place in her life for them.

Creative work changes you. You always grow with it. If you don't, something is wrong. This is true for the actors and writers, too, who work right out of their souls. As an actor said to me once, "You take your guts and lay them right out in front of people. The good thing is, they don't know it's you, they just think it's this character."

I had a uniquely intelligent cast in *Lost in Yonkers*: they were very verbal and had opinions about everything—the movie, the world and politics. Basically, directing, writing and acting are all about having an opinion. If you don't have an opinion, then you can't play the scene. You have to know how you feel. But it's less intellectual than emotional. Intellectualization is not a requirement of a great actor.

For the film, Irene Worth, who plays Grandma, and Mercedes Ruehl, Bella, fully reevaluated the roles they had played so many times on stage. We all knew we couldn't just take the play and put it on the screen, because the screen offers a vastly larger range of expression. Not only can you do the long shots, which resemble the stage, but you can come in close, where a look, even a raised eyebrow, can be bigger than the biggest moment on stage. Many of Bella and Grandma's intimate scenes—like Bella making the bed in the beginning and Grandma making tea at the end—had been huge, loud things on stage because they were reaching for the back row. But now, they could be done like real life, whispered or sitting over a cup of tea and telling secrets.

Sometimes the same things worked in the play and film but for different reasons. At the end of the tea-making scene, after Bella finally confronts Grandma with her rage and makes her face the cost of a lifetime of denials and pain, Irene—alone on the big stage—stuffs her handkerchief into her mouth to stifle a scream. On Broadway, Irene's body language and isolation carried the feeling. But in the film, her face fills the screen and you see the tears well up in her eyes. I wondered if the gesture would work, but its power remains the same.

The last scene between Grandma and Bella was a special challenge because it followed the after-dinner scene, which has all six characters together and a lot of yelling and screaming. The two scenes can't be played the same way in the living room, and they each take up to fifteen pages of the screenplay. So I started the last scene outside, with Irene snapping beans on the back porch. Then we followed her with Bella up the stairs we had constructed for that moment, and through the narrow hall into the kitchen, then into the dining room, and finally into the living room where Grandma ends the scene on her throne-like chair. There are five different locations, and Bella and Grandma move as people would do. The tea-making enabled us to throw away some of the early part of the scene: Irene gets spoons out of a drawer, with her back to us, and crosses to the dining room as Bella asks, "Why did God make me this way?" It builds from a big confrontation to a bigger one.

We shot this and other scenes with steadycam—a camera strapped onto the cameraman who can then follow the action without using dolly tracks. I wanted to make the movie in a contemporary style; I didn't want it to be static. This is a period film, not a laid-back memory piece. Though it's narrated, it's not narrated from anywhere deep in the future: Jay tells the story as it goes along. The in-your-face style the steadycam made possible had to do with the grittiness of the reality and the truth of the emotion. It emphasizes the naturalness of the way people relate to each other.

Two scenes were dictated to me by the material: the scene between Grandma, Eddie and the boys when they first come to the house, and the after-dinner scene when Bella tells the family she wants to marry Johnny. That first scene has to have certain alignments: it's a static scene, which is a challenge in a movie. After all, Grandma with her limp is not going to be running around the room, and the boys have to stand there, uptight, in such stillness you hear the clock ticking. So we animated it with angles and cuts.

A cut creates time and space: this is film theory that's true. People think that if they cut they make it shorter by trimming, but you also add a feeling of time because there is an adjustment in the eye. A lot of cuts and close-ups are very common now, very TV, and I think they assault the audience. I don't believe that character comedy and drama play well in close-up. But in this scene I used close-ups to show nuances of reaction and cuts to make the scene more interesting.

I also had the sun set during this twelve-page scene. This isn't usually done in interiors, but the scene is so long this could actually happen. The idea came to me from the fact that the boys arrive after six o'clock, to a creepy house and a particularly creepy moment when their father has to leave them with Grandma. On a symbolic level, they are going into the darkness of their life. Our cinematographer, Johnny Jensen, built a sunset rig, and during the scene, the warm sunlight sinks and then fades from the side, and the bluer reflected light of dusk comes up. When you start, Grandma enters—blam!—silhouetted in a beam of light from the window and the boys are in spotlights against the dark walls. By the end of the scene, it's dark, and Bella, who insists that the boys stay, turns the light on in the closet to get the blankets to make their bed. Bella is the light, she saves them; Grandma is darkness, like the storm that later drenches them. Nobody will be conscious of this, but it sets up a powerful feeling, like music behind the scene. You will feel it in the film.

The after-dinner scene is the set piece of the play. Everyone is hysterical, and then all of a sudden the play turns on a dime, and you are devastated: the challenge was to make it three-dimensional, to make it move. I broke it down into several sections, as if they were independent scenes, and carefully planned the transition shots between them. In the play, Mercedes's acting alone takes you from the comedy to the drama in an instant. But in a film that performance power does not carry as well as it does on stage, where no one else is moving. In the end, the big moment was filmed the opposite way from what you would expect. Instead of a close-up on Mercedes, we dropped back and showed the whole room. You may not be aware of it, but this lets you reach out to her, while in the play she has to reach out to you. You see her body language—always important with Bella—when she says, "He wants me!"

A few men like to do movies about women, like Ingmar Bergman, but it's rare to find a man interested in exploring female characters from inside. As a woman director, I can bring a kind of insight into women in movies. I'm sure I affected the evolution of Bella's and Grandma's characters, which could have become caricatures. Perhaps with the boys, I brought an appreciation of humor. For women appreciate different things in men than men do, and humor is an important one. (There are a lot of humorless ho-hum heroes around.)

My gender will affect how free people feel with me or how constrained by certain things. It does color every relation on the set. But I dislike generalizing about women—as if we were One Woman—because we are not interchangeable.

I had the classic art-school complex that I was undereducated. That's one of the reasons I am so active in film organizations like the Association of Independent Video and Filmmakers, which I helped found, and the Directors Guild—because we live in a culture that doesn't respect the arts. An artist should not think only of ticket sales or how the economy is doing or whether the deal is right. It's good to reinforce your own identity in the community of artists.

My parents were both architects who trained with Walter Gropius at Harvard, and I was raised among artists in New Haven—the painter Josef Albers and the sculptor Alexander Calder were close friends of the family. The only school in the United States run like the Bauhaus was the Rhode Island School of Design, so I was destined to go there. I eventually got my B.A. in film from RISD, but after I got my M.F.A. in film from New York University's Institute of Film and Television. My résumé is not linear.

In the mid-seventies I decided to go to Hollywood on the basis of *Not a Pretty Picture* and my other documentaries, and I developed projects for Francis Ford Coppola for about four years. During that time I studied with Lee Strasberg and Stella Adler as a director-actor and I interned with the director Robert Wise. When Ray Stark asked me not to print more than a take or two for *Lost in Yonkers*, I understood this, because I had learned the discipline from Wise. That limit used to be a studio rule, an economy measure, and the number of takes chalked on the slate is still a gauge of how you are doing and how fast you're moving on the set. Printing economically is not a problem for me, and you edit the picture more quickly. You do have to be sure of yourself.

Next I am shooting a film for Joe Roth at Caravan with Geena Davis, set in Bensonhurst, Brooklyn, about a girl who gets pregnant and makes all the wrong decisions. It's a comedy drama. I love combining the two, I think life combines the two. Comedy *is* drama. When I had my son, I realized you go through expectation, excitement and pain and incredible joy, and if the baby gets sick, incredible fear. The stuff of *Lost in Yonkers* is the stuff of birth and death—the stuff of life. The rest of it is just filler. I feel entertainment is very important, but life can be fun and tragic, and it all comes at you and you have no control over it. You'd better handle it and have a sense of humor or you'll essentially miss life. You'll be living filler. If you can't take the pain, then you miss the joy. Having a child changed my life.

Martha Coolidge listens as Mike Damus talks about this roof scene with Richard Dreyfuss: the young actor has to manage the transition from comic poker-playing to a serious exchange with the star.

THE SCREENPLAY

NEIL SIMON

Doll hangs by the neck from a string from the rearview mirror.

The credits start

Ext. Road - Day
We see a late 1930's car driving on a country road. It is summer, a hot and sultry day, and the road is dusty. As we follow the car, we hear the voice of Jay Kurnitz, fifteen years old.

JAY (V.O.)
In the summer of 1942, my father drove my brother Arty and me up to Yonkers, New York to visit our grandmother for the first time in two years... Mom died about three months ago, we were at war with Germany and Japan and Pop was nervous because Grandma didn't like him much and the feeling was mutual... This trip had all the signs of a disaster even bigger than Pearl Harbor.

Ext./Int. Car - Day
The father, Eddie Kurnitz, forty, a nervous man prone to hypertension, is driving, with Jay beside him and Arty, thirteen, sprawled out on the back seat. Despite the oppressive heat, they are all wearing suits, shirts and ties.

ARTY
Boy, it's hot. Can I open this window, Pop?

EDDIE
It's broken. Don't fool around with it. It's not my car.

JAY
It would be breezier if we went faster, Pop.

EDDIE
You go faster, you use up more gas. Gas is rationed, there's a war on. Don't bother me.

Ext. Road - Day
We see the car moving along as the credits continue.

Ext. Gas Station - Day
The car pulls in. The gas attendant comes out.

ATTENDANT
What'll it be?

EDDIE
Three gallons.

ATTENDANT
Stamp book?

Eddie hands the book to the attendant.

EDDIE
Is there a bathroom in there?

(Opposite) **Eddie Kurnitz** (Jack Laufer) **and his sons Jay** (Brad Stoll) **and Arty** (Mike Damus)**, whose lives will change when they come to Grandma's house in Yonkers.**

The gas station where Eddie and the boys stop on their way to Grandma's. The truck and signs are older than 1942.

ATTENDANT
Yes, straight through there.

EDDIE
To the boys: I'm going to the bathroom. You can stretch but no playing. It's dusty around here.

They all get out. Arty sees the Coca-Cola cooler.

ARTY
Can we get a Coke, Pop?

EDDIE
Grandma has a candy store, doesn't she? You'll get plenty of soda there.

He heads for the washroom as the boys pick up stones and scale them across the road.

JAY
That's the third time he stopped to pee. That's what Grandma does to him.

ARTY
Makes him pee?

JAY
You know what she used to do to Aunt Bella? Grandma hit her on the head every time Aunt Bella did something stupid. Which only made her stupider. If she dropped a spoon, Whacko! *(he does "Whacko" with his hand)* If she tore her stockings, Whacko!... That's what they used to call her in high school. Whacko!

ARTY
Aunt Bella went to high school?

JAY
A little. She missed the first year because she couldn't find it. *(Arty breaks up laughing)*

On the back steps at Grandma's, Eddie (Jack Laufer) **warns his sons to behave while he talks privately with his fearsome mother.**

Eddie comes out of the washroom, fixing his pants.

EDDIE
Boys, in the dirt.

Ext. Street - Candy Store - Day
The car comes around a street. It is a rural part of Yonkers, not yet built up. Some stores, some empty lots and plenty of trees. This is, after all, 1942. The car passes a corner store and turns. On the window and awning of the store, it says, "Kurnitz's Kandy Store"... Above the store is an apartment where Grandma and Bella live. The car turns into the lot next to the store.

JAY (V.O.)
Even though it was ninety-eight degrees outside, you could feel a chill in the air as we got near the house where Grandma lived... I'm sure glad Arty and I never grew up here.

They get out of the car. Eddie stops and looks up at the second-floor window, a look of foreboding on his face... Then he looks at the boys.

EDDIE
Wipe your face, Arty. You got perspiration all over.

ARTY
She doesn't like sweating?

Eddie gives him a glare. Arty takes out a hanky and wipes his face.

They enter the building through the back door.

Int. House - Back Hallway - Day
They are in the back hallway that leads both to the store and to a stairway that leads up to the apartment.

EDDIE
Alright, you two wait in the store. I have to have a little talk with Grandma first.

Int. Candy Store - Day
He opens the door to the candy store. It is vacant, with the shade pulled down over the front door.

Int. Back Hallway - Day

EDDIE
Don't touch anything in here because Grandma knows where everything is. Not a pretzel, not a Tootsie Roll, nothing, you understand?

JAY
Yes, Pop.

ARTY
Yes, Pop.

EDDIE
I don't know where Aunt Bella is. But don't let her make you anything. If you want ice cream or a soda, Grandma's the one who says yes. Understand?

JAY
Yes, Pop.

ARTY
Yes, Pop.

Storyboard artist Maurice Zuberano's drawing of Grandma's candy store shows its wide windows on the street corner, its tables for soda-fountain patrons and its impressive cash register.

EDDIE
And if you see Aunt Bella, no jokes about her. You hear me?

JAY
I hear you.

ARTY
We hear you.

EDDIE
Alright. I'll call you in a few minutes.

He goes up the stairs. Jay and Arty cross into the candy store.

Int. Candy Store - Day
As they walk in, their faces light up as if discovering the treasure on Treasure Island.

Around the Room
Individual shots of candy. Every kind imaginable. Silver bells, chocolate bars, peanut brittle, licorice sticks, gum, pretzels, etc. On the walls over the soda fountain are pictures of ice cream sodas, milk shakes, sundaes and banana splits.

The boys

ARTY
How could Pop torture us like this? His own kids.

JAY
You touch one thing in here and that German cane'll come flying down the stairs and you'll be back in kindergarten.

ARTY
It would be worth it.

Ext. Street - Day
We see Bella Kurnitz walking down the street. She is in her mid- to late thirties, but has the presence of a sixteen-year old. She is a child in a woman's body and has both an open, warm smile for the world and a nervous, quick cautiousness, either of which can turn on a dime. She carries a purse and a movie magazine. As she walks, she appears lost in thought.

A garbage truck passes by and the driver honks his horn at her and his buddy gives a shrill whistle.

TRUCK DRIVER
Hey, Bella. You wanna make the rounds with us?

BELLA
(haughtily, without looking up at them) I'm not in the garbage business, thank you.

They laugh and drive on.

Ext. The Street - Barbershop - Day
Bella passes a barbershop.

Two tough sixteen-year-'old kids, exchanging a cigarette, stand there, ogling her. They are Danny and Phil.

DANNY
Hey, Bella! Looking pretty snazzy today.

BELLA
(doesn't look or stop) Don't say anything, Bella. Just walk right by them.

DANNY
When we gonna take that little walk down to the river, honey?

BELLA
(stops, turns) Don't you talk that way to me, Danny Petrillo! You little punk kid. You punks should be in school instead of smoking cigarettes... You behave yourselves, you hear me? *(she turns, walks on, then smiles and turns slightly)* ...but thanks for asking.

She walks on.

Int. Candy Store - Close Shot of a Photograph - Day
It is framed, old and faded, hanging on the wall of the candy store. The photo is of the interior of the store as it was twenty-five years ago. We see Grandma Kurnitz in front of the counter, leaning on her cane. A twelve-year old Bella is behind the counter in an apron. There are three other kids in the picture, in various places, posed looking into the camera.

JAY
(pointing) ...This one looks like Pop, this is Uncle Louie, this is Aunt Bella, I guess. Looked a little goofy even then... And this one is Aunt Gert.

ARTY
The one that can't breathe too good?

Arty (Mike Damus) **can look but he's forbidden to touch Grandma's teasingly gorgeous candy.**

JAY

Yeah. Did you ever notice that there is something wrong with everyone on Pop's side of the family? Mom told me that.

ARTY

How come Aunt Gert can't breathe?

JAY

I don't know. She can't... She can't talk right. She says the first half of a sentence breathing out and the second half sucking in. You've seen it.

ARTY

Do it for me.

JAY

Pop'll hear it. He said no jokes, didn't he?

ARTY

Only about Aunt Bella. Come on. Show me how Aunt Gert sucks in her sentences.

JAY

(glances upstairs first, then to Arty, imitating Aunt Gert's voice) "Oh, hello, Jay. How are you? How's your father? And how's—*(sucks breath in)*—your little brother, Arty?"

ARTY

(gets hysterical) I love it. I love it when you do that.

JAY

I once saw her try to blow out a candle and halfway there, she sucked it back on.

Arty gets hysterical and falls back on the floor. We suddenly see Bella outside the window, walking by the store. Jay notices her.

JAY

Hey! There's Aunt Bella.

Arty sits up.

JAY

Where's she going?

ARTY

Probably forgot where she lives.

Jay rushes to the front door and opens it. Arty comes up beside him.

JAY

Aunt Bella? Where are you going?

Ext. The Street - Day
Bella stops when she hears Jay.

BELLA

What?

JAY

Aren't you coming in?

BELLA

(looks around puzzled) I'm glad you caught me. I was daydreaming. I would have walked right into the ocean.

She comes into the store. The boys follow and close the door.

Int. Candy Store - Day

BELLA

What are you kids doing in here? It's after six o'clock. We're closed.

Jay and Arty look at each other.

JAY

It's Jay and Arty, Aunt Bella... your nephews.

She looks at them, stunned.

BELLA

...Oh, my God! It's Jay and Arty! My nephews... I thought you were coming out on Saturday.

JAY

It is Saturday.

BELLA

I know that... Jay and Arty! Oh, it's so good to see you. Give your Aunt Bella a kiss. Come here, you.

She pulls them into her arms and kisses them both.

BELLA

(squints) Come on outside. I want to get a better look at you. C'mon. I want to see how big you both got.

She rushes for back door.

Int. Back Hallway - Day
She runs down the back hallway, followed by the boys.

Ext. Back Porch - Day
She sits on the swing bench. The boys come out.

BELLA

Stand there! ...No, no, no...there... In size places.

They switch places.

BELLA

Oh, you've both got so much bigger. You're growing up so fast, it almost makes me cry. Where's your father? I haven't seen your father in so long.

ARTY

He's upstairs talking to Grandma.

BELLA

(suddenly nervous) Oh. I better not disturb them... Did she ask for me?

JAY

I don't know.

BELLA

Did you tell her I was here?

JAY

No. You just got here.

BELLA

Did you tell her where I went?

JAY

We didn't know where you went.

BELLA

I went to the movies. *(she puts her fingers to her lips)* Don't tell Grandma. I saw that picture with Bette Davis and George Brent. You know the one?

ARTY

No.

BELLA

It was with Bette Davis and George Brent. Oh, oh. And they had air-conditioning. I was actually cold. I felt so happy for the actors to be in an air-conditioned theater.

Jay and Arty look at each other.

JAY

I don't think the actors feel it. They're just pictures on the screen.

BELLA

Oh, I know that, silly. I mean they'd be happy to know that people who were watching the movie were nice and cool so we enjoyed the movie better.

JAY

Oh. Right.

ARTY

Sure.

BELLA

I bet I know what would make you two cool in a second. What about a great big ice-cream sundae deluxe with everything on it. Yes. Come on. I'll make 'em for you.

She gets up and goes into the house.

JAY

No wait, wait... Arty, Arty.

Int. Candy Store - Day
Bella comes in, followed by the boys.

JAY

The thing is, Pop said we shouldn't have anything yet, right, Arty?

ARTY

I don't remember.

Bella crosses behind the soda fountain.

BELLA

Oh, your father. He never takes anything from anybody. *(she puts an apron on)* I couldn't even give your mother a cup of coffee. Did you know that? *(she gets two sundae glasses down)* Where is your mother anyway?

JAY

(confused) She's dead. Mom is dead.

That stops Bella for a moment, but not for long.

BELLA

Yeah, I know, I know. I mean where is she buried?

JAY

At Mount Israel Cemetery in the Bronx. You were at the funeral, remember?

BELLA

You mean the first time?

JAY

What do you mean, the first time?

BELLA

When I came in the car, not the bus.

ARTY

The bus?

BELLA

Oh! No! No! No! That was somebody else. Sometimes my mind wanders. The kids at school used to say, "Hey, Bella, Lost and Found called and said 'Come get your brains'..." *(she laughs)* Except, I really didn't think that was so funny.

She starts to make the two ice-cream sundaes. She's very fast, very generous with her portions and very professional with her work. Arty and Jay watch with amazement.

BELLA

(as she works) Yeah, I was really sad about your mother. Oh boy, I bet you miss her... It's such a shame she couldn't have had more children. She didn't, did she?

JAY

No.

BELLA

No. *(puts sprinkles and nuts on in a design)* My mother had six children, did you know that? There was me, your father, Louie and Gert...and Aaron and Rose, who died when they were both very little. And in between, my father died, when my mother was pregnant with me... Is that all right to say to boys?

JAY

Yeah, sure.

BELLA

So, I never met my father but boy...I still loved him. Because I just knew he would have taken care of me the way your father takes care of you. You know what I mean?

JAY

Right.

BELLA

Yeah. *(she perks up)* So how old do you think I am? Take a guess. Arty? C'mon.

ARTY

I don't know. About thirty-five?

BELLA

Thirty-five? Wrong. You are so wrong. You are so far off it's not even funny... I'm thirty-six. And I don't even look it, do I?

ARTY

No.

BELLA

No... So, two deluxe hot fudge sundaes with everything on them.

She puts the two sundaes on the counter with napkins and spoons and wipes off the counter with a flourish.

BELLA

Dig in, boys.

Arty picks up his spoon, about to dig in. Jay stops him.

JAY

Like I said, Pop didn't want us to have anything yet. He didn't want to upset Grandma. We really should wait.

BELLA

What do you mean, wait? They're done. They're starting to melt already. Look at Arty drooling.

JAY

We really do want them. It's just that Pop said.

BELLA

No wait, no wait. This is the last time I'm asking. Yes or no. This is the final call.

Arty looks at Jay who returns a cool glance.

ARTY

(to Bella) ...Maybe later.

BELLA

(snaps coldly, angrily) No! Not later! It's too late!!

She takes the two sundaes and dumps them into the sink. Arty looks horrified.

(more dialogue but it is inaudible under the sound of dumping the sundaes.)

BELLA

You just hurt my feelings, the both of you. *(she rips off her apron)* I know that you miss your mother but that's no reason you can be disrespectful to me. *(she comes out from behind the counter)* I loved your mother always, whether she took coffee from me or not and you can tell your father that for me. *(she heads for front door)* I am so sick of this. I'm j-j-j-ust...I'm sick of this.

Bella (Mercedes Ruehl) **proudly presents the best sundaes she can make.**

She goes out the door and slams it hard. She stands in the street against the window, sulking with her arms folded and biting her thumbnail backwards.

JAY
(to Arty) You see why I don't like to come here too much?

Top of the Stairs
The door opens and Eddie comes out. There's a flight of stairs from upstairs that leads into the candy store as well.

EDDIE
Where's Aunt Bella? I thought I just heard her.

ARTY
(points out to street) She's out there.

We see Bella biting away at her thumbnail.

EDDIE
(coming down the stairs) Is she alright?

JAY
How do I know when she's alright?

EDDIE
Hey! Hey, I told you no remarks about Aunt Bella. (he crosses to the door)
Now go upstairs and wait for me. We have to talk. Go on…move.

Bella is overjoyed to see her brother Eddie (Jack Laufer).

He crosses out the door.

Ext. Street - Candy Store - Day
Eddie goes out and crosses to Bella.

EDDIE
Bella! You okay, honey?

BELLA
All I wanted to do was make them happy. They had no right to treat me that way. *(recognizing him)* Eddie! Eddie! *(she throws her arms around him)* It's so good to see you. *(she kisses him)*

EDDIE
It's good to see you too, Bella. Listen, honey, Momma needs you to rub her legs. They're hurting again.

BELLA
No, she doesn't. They only hurt when I come home.

EDDIE
No, no, no, honey, be nice to her. Please. Especially today.

BELLA
Can we have a talk?

EDDIE
Yes, promise.

BELLA
A long one.

EDDIE
A long one after you're done.

Ext. House - Late Day
We are on a long shot of the house. We hear Jay's voice-over.

JAY (V.O.)
...And then we had our talk with Pop. He told us how he had gone broke spending all his money on Mom's hospital bills... And then he told us he got a job selling scrap iron to build ships and tanks...and that maybe he could make back the nine thousand dollars in just a year.

Int. Living Room - Day
The boys are sitting on the sofa, listening intently as Eddie paces, continuing his story.

EDDIE
...The factories I would sell to are in the South. Kentucky, Louisiana, Texas. I'd be gone about ten months, staying in hotels, buses, trains. Anyplace I could find a room. And we'd be free and clear in less than a year.

JAY
That's great, Pop.

EDDIE
So, now the question comes, where do you two live while I'm gone?

Jay and Arty are dumbstruck.

ARTY
(wipes brow) God, it's hot in here.

JAY
Please, Pop. Don't make us live here. That's what you're thinking, isn't it?

EDDIE
I have no choice. I gave the apartment up today.

ARTY
You gave it up?

EDDIE
The landlady raised the rent. Everybody's looking to make money out of this war.

JAY
Grandma wouldn't be happy with us. We're slobs. And Arty's always breaking things.

ARTY
Remember when I broke the good water pitcher? And the ink stains on the sofa? All mine. I'm dangerous, Pop.

EDDIE
Listen to me, both of you. Now, she hasn't said yes positively yet. She's old, set in her ways. And she's worried about people being around Bella.

ARTY
Me too.

EDDIE
She'll come out, she'll talk to you boys, and see how it goes. If she says no, I can't take this job. It's up to you boys to convince her that you won't be any trouble. And that you really want to live here. Can you do that?

The boys look at each other.

Bella suddenly rushes into the room with a towel, crying.

BELLA
Eddie! Eddie!

She reaches out for him

EDDIE
(takes her in his arms) What, what, what?

BELLA
She's so mean to me.

EDDIE
No, no, she's not. She's just old.

BELLA
Can't you come and live with us, I miss you so much.

EDDIE
I can't, honey. I have to go away for a while. But I have some good news for you, sweetheart. You know who's going to stay here? If Momma says "yes"?... Arty and Jay. Won't that be nice?

BELLA
Yes.

Bella looks at them and nods and smiles a very big yes. Jay and Arty just look blank.

EDDIE
...Momma's thinking about it now. So why don't you lay down in your room for a while, Bella?

BELLA
(grabs his hand) No, no, no. I want to stay here with you.

EDDIE
I would be easier if Momma and the boys talked alone, Bella.

BELLA
(sternly) I'm staying with you.

EDDIE
(losing composure) Oh, God! Alright. Okay. Here you sit down right here. *(points to chair in corner of the room)* But you got to be very quiet. We don't want to get Momma upset.

She moves chair in corner.

EDDIE
Okay. Fix your tie, Jay. Straighten your collar, Arty.

They do, quickly.

EDDIE
Stand up straight, both of you.

They stand like ramrods, hands straight at their sides.

Eddie crosses to Grandma's door and knocks.

EDDIE
Momma? Okay?

He backs up.

The Doorknob

It slowly turns.

Boys' faces

Their eyes have terror in them.

The Door

It opens and Grandma comes out.

(Opposite) **Eddie** (Jack Laufer) **tells his sons he must leave them with Grandma: he has to take a traveling salesman's job to pay off his late wife's hospital bills and he has let their apartment go.**

Waiting for Grandma's dramatically delayed entrance, Arty (Mike Damus, left) **and Jay** (Brad Stoll) **stand up straight, as if for a firing squad. They must persuade her to take them in.**

This is the first full view of Grandma we have seen. She appears to be big, at least to the boys. She is full-bosomed, wearing a dull print dress, steel-framed glasses, walks with a decided limp, aided by her infamous cane. Her hair is gray-white, with braids tied in a bun at the back.

She is about seventy-five. There is not an ounce of warmth or compassion about her. She crosses wordlessly to her favorite chair, takes her time sitting and then looks up at the boys for the first time... She waits before she says anything.

GRANDMA
...So?

Eddie motions with his head to the boys.

JAY
(on cue, slight bow) Hello, Grandma.

Eddie quickly gives them another head signal and they both quickly cross to Grandma, bend over and kiss her on the cheek. She turns her head away from their eyes. They step back a few feet.

EDDIE
I know you haven't seen the boys in a long time, Mom. They wanted to come but their mother was so sick. They've grown up, haven't they?

GRANDMA
(points cane at Arty) Dis is da little one?

EDDIE
Yes. Arthur. He's two years younger than Jay.

GRANDMA
(looks at Jay) Dis one I remember more. Dis one looks like his mother. *(says this like it's an insult to Jay)* Vot's da matter with your eyes.

JAY
My eyes? Nothing. I have a little allergy.

GRANDMA
You were crying maybe?

JAY
Me? No. I never cry.

GRANDMA
Big boys shouldn't cry.

JAY
I know. I haven't cried in years. A couple of times when I was a baby, though.

EDDIE
They're strong kids, Ma. Both of them.

GRANDMA
(to Jay) Yakob, heh?

JAY
Yeah. But they call me Jay.

GRANDMA
No. I don't like Jay. Yakob is a name.

JAY
Sure. Yakob is fine.

GRANDMA
(looks at Arty) And Artur.

ARTY
Arthur. But they call me Arty.

GRANDMA
I don't call you Arty.

ARTY
Sure. I love Arthur. Like King Arthur.

GRANDMA
You go to school?

ARTY
Yeah.

GRANDMA
Vot?

ARTY
Yes. I go to the same school as Yakob.

Arty (Mike Damusl) **becomes Artur for Grandma, the German-Jewish refugee played by Irene Worth, and gives her a dutiful kiss.**

EDDIE

He's wiping his brow.

GRANDMA
Vich is da smart one?

EDDIE
They both do very well in school.

GRANDMA
No, no, no. Dey will tell me. *(to boys)* Vich one is da smart one?

The boys look at each other.

ARTY
Yakob is. He gets A's in everything. I'm better at sports.

GRANDMA
Shports?

ARTY
Baseball. Football.

GRANDMA
You play in da mud? You come home with filthy shoes and make marks all over da floor?

ARTY
No. Never. I clean them off at the field. I bring a brush and polish and shine them up on a bench.

He looks at Eddie to see if he got away with that one.

GRANDMA
So tell me... Vy do you want to live with Grandma?

They all look at each other.

ARTY
Why don't you tell Grandma, Yakob?

JAY
Well—because—when Pop said we had the opportunity to live here with you, our only living Grandmother, and our only living Aunt Bella... Well, I thought that families should sort of stick together now that our country is at war with Germ—Japan... and that... er... Oh... I also think that—No. That's all.

He crosses to sofa and sits.

GRANDMA
(to Eddie) And dis is da smart one?

EDDIE
I thought he said that very well, Momma.

GRANDMA
(points cane at Arty) And vot about dis King Artur... Vy do you vant to liff with Grandma?

ARTY
Because we have no place else to go.

EDDIE
Arty!!!

GRANDMA
No, no, no. He knows what he vants to say. I tink maybe diss one is da smart one...

Bella sits wordlessly entranced in this conversation, her chin cupped in her hands.

GRANDMA
Alright... alright... So now Grandma will tell you vy she doesn't think you should live with her... Dis house is no place for boys. I'm an old woman. I don't like noise. I don't like people in my house. I had six children once, I don't need more again....

EDDIE
Momma, can I just say something?

GRANDMA
(to the boys) No, I just say something... Vy should I do this? Vot do I owe your father? Ven did he ever come around here after he married your mother? I never saw him. She turned him against me. His own mother. She didn't like me, I didn't like her. I'm not afraid to tell the truth either... He cried in my bedroom. Not like a man, like a child he cried. He was always that way. I buried a husband and two children und I didn't cry. I didn't have time... Bella vas born with scarlet fever und until she was five years old, she didn't talk. Und I didn't cry. Her sister Gertrude can't talk without choking und I didn't cry. Und maybe one day dey'll find Louie dead in da street and I von't cry. Dot's how I was raised. To be strong. You don't survive in this world without being like steel... You think I'm cruel? You think I'm a terrible person? Dot a grandmother should talk like dis? Goot! Make you hard. Make you strong! Den you learn how to take care of yourselves. Und you don't need anybody's help. So dot's my decision. Maybe some day you'll thank me.

She pushes herself up with her cane, heads for the door.

GRANDMA
Give da boys an ice-cream cone, Bella. Den come inside and rub my legs.

They are all stunned. Bella seems impervious to Grandma's cruelty.

EDDIE
You're right, Momma. I am the weak one. The crybaby... But you're wrong about one thing. Evelyn never turned me against you. She turned me towards her. To loving. To caring. I am sorry now about not bringing the boys out here more. Maybe the reason I didn't was because I was afraid they'd learn something here that I tried to forget. Maybe they just learned it today... Never mind the ice cream-cones, Bella. Maybe some other time. *(he crosses to door)* Come on, boys. We're going.

The boys are still transfixed.

EDDIE
I said let's go.

Bella jumps up from her seat.

BELLA

Arty? We'll have dinner another night, okay? Why don't you and Jay go home and pack your things and I'll get your beds ready.

The boys look at Eddie. Bella goes to closet and pulls out pillows.

EDDIE

Thank you anyway, Bella, but Momma and I just decided it wasn't a very good idea.

Bella puts pillows on table, then pulls out the bed from the sofa. She gets a blanket from the closet.

BELLA

(to boys) And don't forget your toothbrushes because we don't carry them in the store. And each of you bring something from your house you really love, even if it's big, and we'll find someplace to put it.

She keeps working fast.

GRANDMA

Bella, dot's enough. Dis is not your business.

BELLA

(to boys, as she makes bed) What about a picture of your mother? We can put it right here. See? And then that will be the last thing that you see at night and the first thing that you see in the morning... Oh, this is so exciting.

She keeps working.

Grandma (Irene Worth, right) **is drill sergeant to the boys on their own home front—the candy store, with its daily chores and forbidden treats.**

GRANDMA

Bella! *(bangs cane on floor)* Nicht sprechen! Enough! They're going. Dot's the end of it.

BELLA

(finishing bed) No, Momma. They're not going. They're staying. Because if you make them go, I'll go too. I know I've said that a thousand times but this time I mean it. I could go to the Home. The Home would take me. You're always telling me that... And if I go, you gonna be all alone. And you're scared to be alone. Nobody knows that but me. But you don't have to be, Momma. Cause we're all gonna be here together. *(the bed is finished)* You and me and Jay and Arty. Won't that be fun?

She is beaming like a child. Grandma is shocked.

We suddenly hear a loud train whistle. It looks like it comes out of Grandma's mouth

Ext./Int. A Train Moving Along - Day
We are somewhere deep in the Southeast. From outside the train, we see Eddie in a window seat. He is writing. We pan along the train and then to the scenery of the South.

JAY

"Dear Pop, Well, we finished our first week with Grandma and we're still alive... Glad you liked Washington, D.C... If you happen to see Abraham Lincoln there, ask him to free the slaves in Yonkers... Just Kidding..."

Montage of Various Shots - Day

Ext. Candy Store - Day
Boys washing the windows of the store.

Ext. Backyard - Day
Boys lugging huge garbage cans out the back door.

Int. Candy Store - Day
Grandma ever present, ever demanding, berating them. Jay drops a box of gumballs all over the floor.

Int. Movie Theater - Night
We are on the screen. We are watching the ending of a Bette Davis movie.

Int. Movie Theater - Bella - Night
She is seated in the audience, watching the film intensely, mouthing Bette Davis's words in unison. The picture ends. The lights come up. The audience files out. Among the older audience, all the younger men seem to be in uniforms. Bella sees one sailor kissing a girl in the next row. She smiles, blushes and puts her head down.

The audience files out. Bella seems to lag behind. We see an usher sweeping up with a broom and valet. His name is Johnny. He is about forty years old and sweet-looking.

BELLA
Hi, Johnny.

JOHNNY
Hi, Bella. Did you like the picture?

The "A.I.A" after David Chapman's name in the credits means he is a member of the American Institute of Architects, a prestigious national accreditation like A.M.A. standing for doctors; he earned his degree in architecture from Georgia Tech. In 1992 Chapman completed the production design for *Mad Dog and Glory*, and previously he created the period styles of *Last Exit to Brooklyn*, *Dirty Dancing*, and *This is My Life*, among other films. On Broadway he designed the revivals of *Cabaret* and *Zorba*, as well as Zoë Caldwell's *Othello* and Martin Charnin's *The First*.

THE DESIGN OF "YONKERS"

When *Lost in Yonkers* moved from Broadway to Hollywood, the world of the Kurnitz family literally opened up, for the film could show what the play could only tell about. Grandma's living room, the single set in the theater production, is now one of a half-dozen interiors, and the diverse locations help define the characters. The film's time, place, and style are the same as the play's. This is 1942. Yonkers, New York. A real family, their world.

David Chapman describes how his production design worked to make this convincing.

"Of course we would have liked to shoot in Yonkers, but it doesn't look the way it did in 1942. Not many American towns do. But in the Midwest there are a few remnants. Ludlow, Kentucky, and Wilmington, Ohio—little towns outside Cincinnati—are more intact than most. We liked them from the minute we got off the airplane.

"Because the high point of Bella's life is getting away to the movies, the movie theater had to be a very special building. We asked the National Historic Register about movie theaters within an hour of Cincinnati, and we looked at the one in Wilmington and then fell in love with the town.

"In Wilmington, which becomes the upscale part of Yonkers for the film, a lot is in pristine condition. Other than adding the awnings and changing the signs, hiding parking meters and taking down TV antennas, which are always necessary, we didn't need to do much. All in all, we redressed ten storefronts in Ludlow, twenty-five in Wilmington.

"In Ludlow we needed to build the candy store and Grandma's apartment above it from scratch. This building is the heart and soul of the movie, as it was in the play. Everything else in the film is there to give us places to go and to propel the story.

"Naturally the screenplay has an enormous number of requirements about the candy store. It has to be on a street corner, of a certain size, with a backyard and a logical place nearby where the kids can crawl through a tunnel and escape. For the roof scenes there could be forty to forty-five people up there, including camera, lights and crew.

"So we rented a corner of a parking lot, and we built the candy store there, sinking concrete footings and giving the store interior an uninterrupted thirty-foot span so the camera could move freely.

"We considered construction in the studio, but we would have had to build not just the candy store but everything around it, a half a city block in each direction. Because we wanted to be able to see out of the windows, watch cars and people going by, be able to do scenes in and out of the store in one take. That kind of construction affects costs. Anyway, the studio can't give you what you get on location, where the concrete curbs are strange, and the sidewalks are uneven and the trees look more real. It's endless the things you can't do in the studio. So we opted to work around Cincinnati, where there's an established Film Commission and they're accustomed to filmmakers.

"We imagined Grandma's house was built in the 1890s and then turned into a candy store around 1905 or 1906. Both the exterior and interior have history. Inside are things she has owned for decades. When I do a period picture, I like to set it even earlier to establish a sense of history.

"Our canvas was 1942; our painting was the particular world of *Lost in Yonkers*. We didn't try to call attention to the design. Rather, we executed the painting as the visual vehicle for the story."

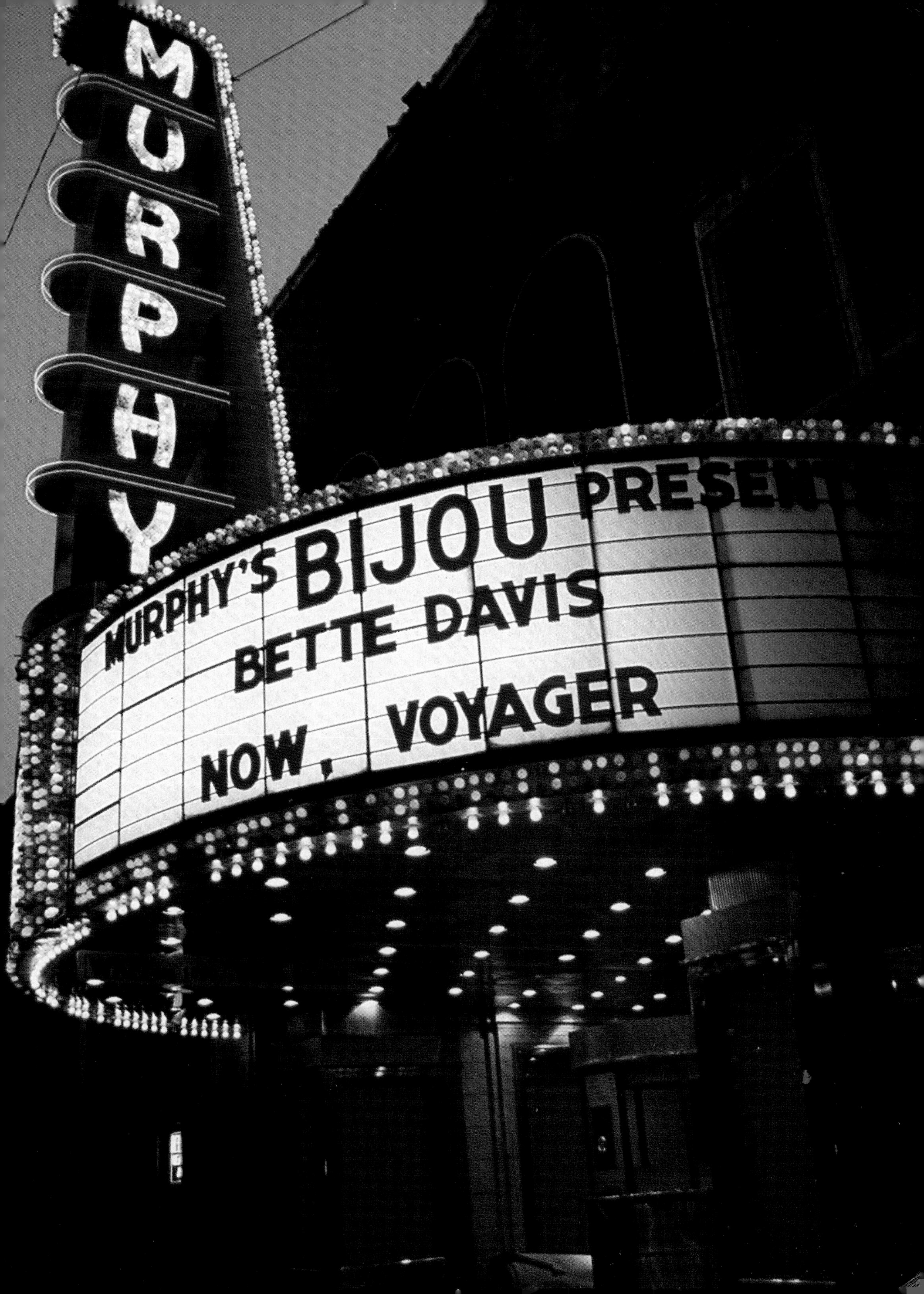
MURPHY
MURPHY'S BIJOU PRESEN
BETTE DAVIS
NOW, VOYAGER

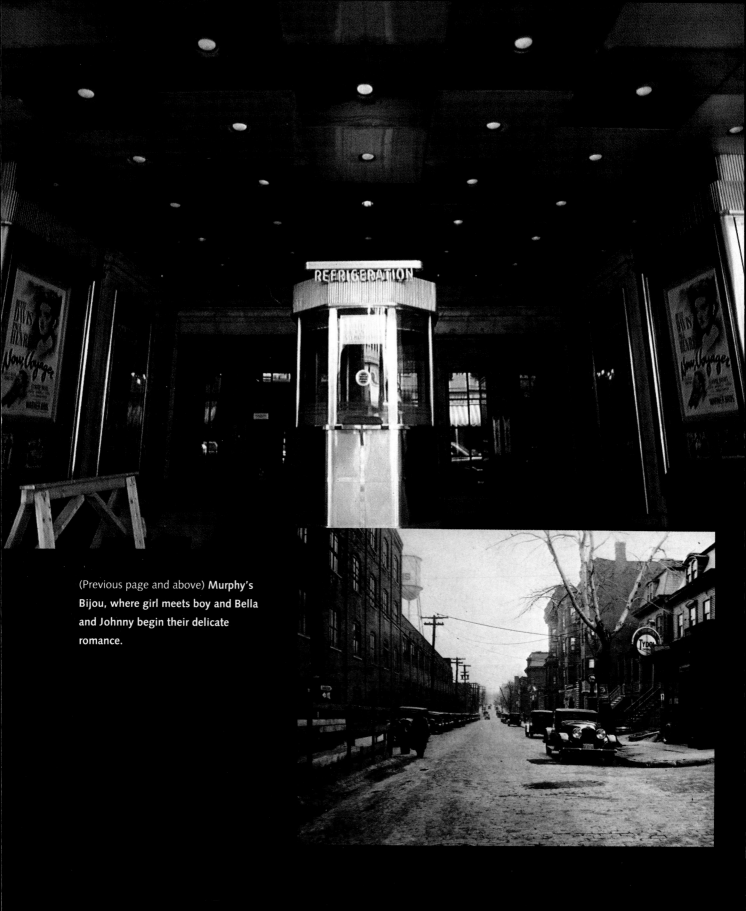

(Previous page and above) **Murphy's Bijou**, where girl meets boy and Bella and Johnny begin their delicate romance.

observes. "Both are hilly, on major rivers—the Hudson and the Ohio—and both started really growing at the turn of the century, so they have a lot of Victorian-style architecture. The people in Ludlow seem to have had a combination of practicality and respect for their structures: when a building changed hands and function, they didn't tear it down, but reused it in its original form. Perhaps it's part of the tradition of this originally German region."

Bella (Mercedes Ruehl) **presents "deluxe hot fudge sundaes with everything on them" to her nephews, Jay and Arty** (Brad Stoll and Mike Damus).

"The challenge of the design was a built-in contradiction in the script," David Chapman comments. *"To the boys, the candy store is a world of total delight, but it's ruled by a very strict grandmother. We had to contrast the bright sugar candies of any kid's heaven with the place that's in part Bella's prison. The building has overtones of a bunker, yet stays true to Victorian architecture. Everything is angular, square and hard-edged—a little off-putting."*

A production design staffer discovered Ray Broekel's The Great American Candy Bar Book in a Cincinnati library and tracked down the author, a voracious collector of candy wrappers, boxes, etc., who generously lent samples to the production team. They scanned the wrappers into a computer, color corrected and/or repaired them as necessary, then printed them through a color Xerox process. Then the set dressing department hand-wrapped hundreds of them around fake candy bars and boxes. In the film, will you notice the period candy? Says David Chapman, "Someone would—if it were wrong!"

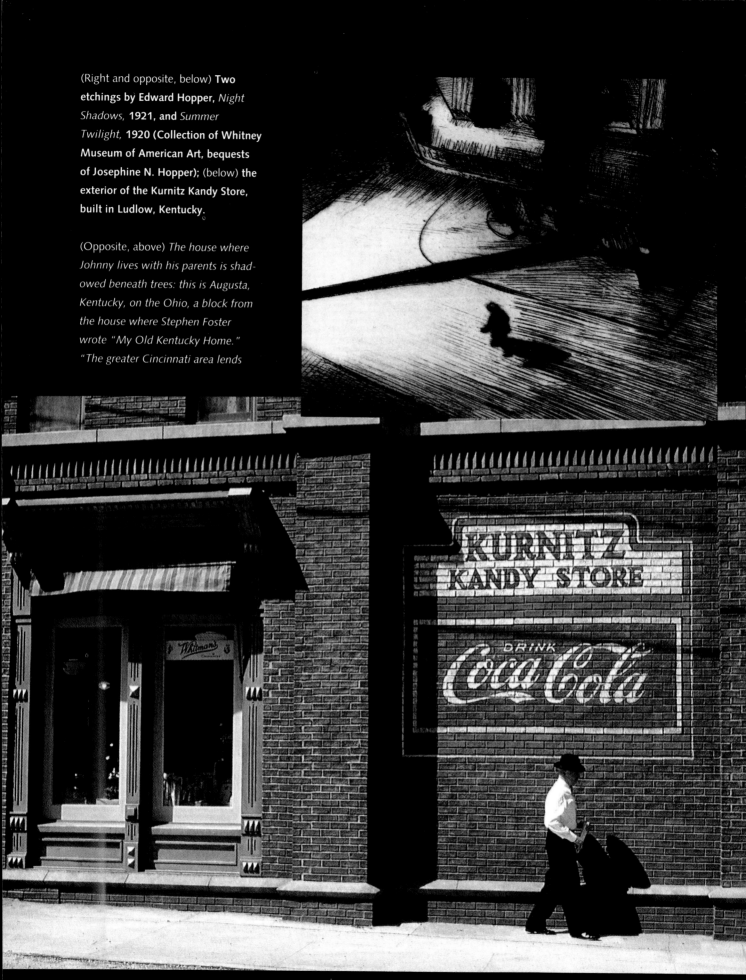

(Right and opposite, below) **Two etchings by Edward Hopper,** *Night Shadows,* **1921, and** *Summer Twilight,* **1920 (Collection of Whitney Museum of American Art, bequests of Josephine N. Hopper); (below) the exterior of the Kurnitz Kandy Store, built in Ludlow, Kentucky.**

(Opposite, above) *The house where Johnny lives with his parents is shadowed beneath trees: this is Augusta, Kentucky, on the Ohio, a block from the house where Stephen Foster wrote "My Old Kentucky Home."* *"The greater Cincinnati area lends*

itself to a wide variety of periods and locations," remarks producer Ray Stark. "We were able to shoot scenes of the Northeast, as well as the deep South, without having to travel very far. The middle-America locale seemed to verify our feelings about the theme of Lost in Yonkers that Neil's story of relations was a universal one, as comfortable in Kentucky as in New York." The film was the tenth shot in Greater Cincinnati since 1987. (The Public Eye, Rain Man and others used the city's downtown and suburbs.) The Yonkers location shooting took five weeks; Chapman spent thirteen weeks supervising a crew of about eighty for preproduction.

A street in Wilmington, Ohio, wears
some new awnings and waits in the
August sun to play its part as back-

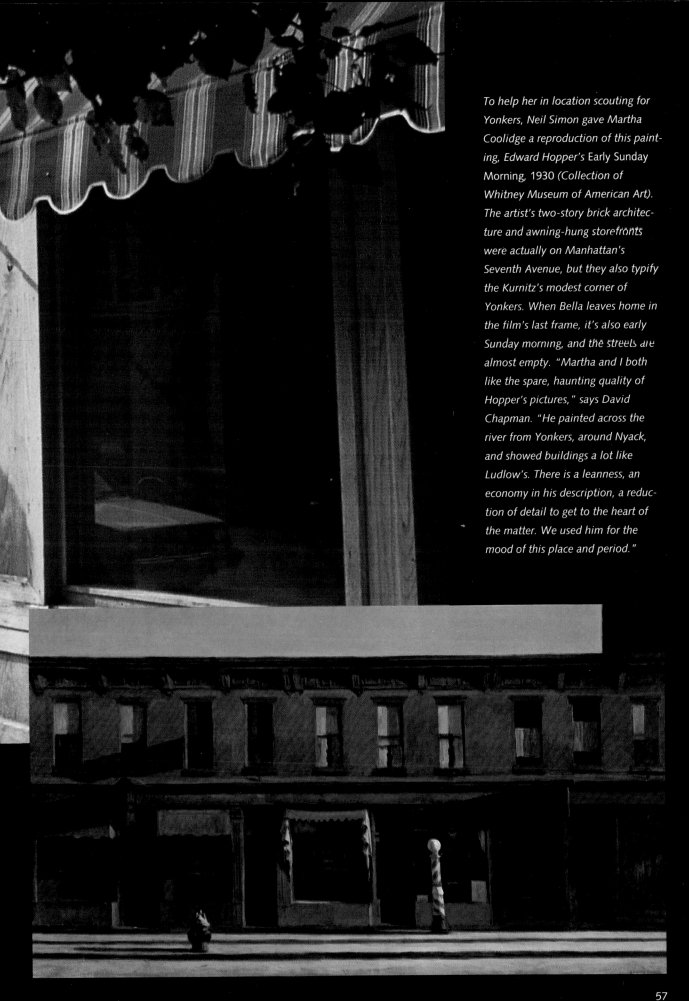

To help her in location scouting for Yonkers, Neil Simon gave Martha Coolidge a reproduction of this painting, Edward Hopper's Early Sunday Morning, 1930 (Collection of Whitney Museum of American Art). The artist's two-story brick architecture and awning-hung storefronts were actually on Manhattan's Seventh Avenue, but they also typify the Kurnitz's modest corner of Yonkers. When Bella leaves home in the film's last frame, it's also early Sunday morning, and the streets are almost empty. "Martha and I both like the spare, haunting quality of Hopper's pictures," says David Chapman. "He painted across the river from Yonkers, around Nyack, and showed buildings a lot like Ludlow's. There is a leanness, an economy in his description, a reduction of detail to get to the heart of the matter. We used him for the mood of this place and period."

"There is a progression from the green prison of the candy store to the movie palace and the livelier world of Wilmington, and the hues get brighter and brighter. You don't follow this schematic design or Bella step by step, but it's felt psychologically. Our goal was to create an idea of the period, but not to belabor it. To make the story real, as if it were happening today, I didn't want anything so interesting or so beautiful or, God help us, so inaccurate that it would detract from the audience's involvement with these people. Our work is like a very good score: it becomes background. You may be aware of it, but it never intrudes."

"We tried to avoid the honey-soaked look of conventional period pictures, the lab look of sepia photographs. We worked instead with warm greens, and eliminated all blue, which is a violently reactive color to film and can produce rogue reflections in odd places. With an almost army-like khaki green in the candy store, the other hues count as real saturated colors. This is a world of severity and magic."

—David Chapman

Hollywood Harry's slick suit, sketched by costume designer Shelley Komarov.

To animate the streets of Yonkers, executive producer Joe Caracciolo imported some fifty period vehicles and transportation coordinator Joe Orlebeck choreographed them, from Depression-era flivvers to the gangsters' white Packard, the only jazzy car among the sober Fords and Chevies of working-class Yonkers. The goal of this abundance was realism, according to production designer David Chapman: with few cars and repeated use of them, you might notice the same one rolling down the block and be distracted from the film.

Hollywood Harry (Robert Guy Miranda) **pays Jay** (Brad Stoll) **a buck to tell him when his "henchman" Uncle Louie comes around.**

On a crane in Ludlow, the director and her cinematographer, Johnny Jensen, have a green light to film Eddie and the boys driving to Grandma's. Jensen shot Coolidge's *Rambling Rose* and won a Spirit Award Nomination for best cinematography on an independently produced film.

"Today if you buy a book, you can become a producer, if you are a lawyer, an agent, or a studio executive, or a line producer, you can become a producer, so many producers know only a portion of the business," Martha Coolidge remarks. "But Ray Stark knows filmmaking. He has made over two hundred films—the experience level is enormous. He'd ask me a question, I'd answer it, he'd say, Oh. Yes. Or, I don't like this. I'd say I don't like it either, let's do something about it. Boom! Done! I got into his speed. I like speedy people, and quick, effective ways of dealing with things. Neil's ability to rewrite in a short time, his understanding, his knowledge of his characters, of what kinds of jokes work and don't—it was all remarkable. We had a tremendous experience of exploring the material together and over again. It was great on his part: he was willing to reconceive it."

Producer Ray Stark (right) **jokes with Martha Coolidge and Richard Dreyfuss on the candy store roof.** (Below) **During a break in location filming, author Neil Simon counsels Brad Stoll and Mike Damus on their crossword puzzle.**

"I've been fortunate to work with great directors in film—Jonathan Demme, Terry Gilliam, and now Martha Coolidge. They are all people who are sensitive to the actor's problems, sensitive to language, and very visual. They are painting pictures, forming compositions, they know the power of this visual medium. What they see in the light and color is immediately translatable into emotion. I saw that in Rambling Rose—*that's why I was so excited when I heard Martha was going to direct* Lost in Yonkers."

—Mercedes Ruehl

RICHARD DREYFUSS AS UNCLE LOUIE

Richard Dreyfuss has collaborated before with writer Neil Simon and producer Ray Stark with notable success: in 1977 the popular and critically esteemed performer won the Academy Award for Best Actor in *The Goodbye Girl*. In *Lost in Yonkers* he obviously relishes his role: "You get to play a gangster and talk like a gangster," he says, "and wear vests and have guns and talk to kids—it's fun."

The film expands an intrinsically plummy role with a chase subplot of semi-comic threat that finally turns serious. Louie's cat-and-mouse game with Hollywood Harry dramatizes his scrappy character, his bravado and defiance. "Louie is the stronger of Grandma Kurnitz's two sons," says Neil Simon. "Grandma's treatment broke Eddie, but it made Louie tough. That's what he learned from her. He lives in Yonkers in a poor lower-middle-class neighborhood, where the quickest way to make a dollar is to steal it. And he became a thief, but a petty thief—a bag man. The mob there takes money from the neighborhood for betting numbers and so on, and Louis collects it and gives the bag to a higher-up, and they probably pay him $25 a week. In the piece, Louis, knowing he's going in the army, decides to keep the bag. The hoodlums wait outside Grandma's to get their money back."

"Louie and his nephews are thrust together in this week of domestic drama," Richard Dreyfuss comments. "He likes the idea that he can spend some time with them and maybe influence them to become little Louies. They're enamored of him, he's a romantic figure in their eyes. They don't realize he's a third-rate gangster.

"In surviving Grandma, her own children have become damaged people in different ways. Louie has become her fierce opponent—a direct result of his upbringing. He is always his mother's son, he reflects her outlook. He has much more charm and humanness than she does, but beneath that is his mother. Angry and capable of violence."

"Toughness, the ability to flout danger—whether from a gangster or from Grandma—is what Louis teaches the boys," Neil Simon adds. "That's something they've never seen in their father and didn't know existed—except maybe in the movies."

Playing movie mobsters is no novelty for Dreyfuss: at the beginning of his film career he first "made a splash" (as Louie would put it) portraying Baby Face Nelson in John Milius's *Dillinger*.

"When I saw Richard for the first time in his costume and mustache and hat," says Martha Coolidge, "he knocked me over. Does he not look like a forties movie star? An actor in a forties movie? He's so manly, such a tough guy. He brought a zing into everything. I asked him about those bits which recall Cagney, George Raft, Brando and other mobster roles, and he said there was no intentional parody. He had intuitively developed a character who's extremely influenced by the movies. The same with Bella—these are people whose ultimate escape from Grandma's house is the movie theater."

Performances by Dreyfuss have filled theaters since he began acting in Los Angeles at age nine. From the late sixties, he played stage and television roles, and he reached big-screen prominence in *American Graffiti* and *The Apprenticeship of Duddy Kravitz*, in which he starred. In the seventies hits for Dreyfuss included *Jaws* and *Close Encounters of the Third Kind*. In the late seventies-early eighties, he alternated between theater and films, performing in *Julius Caesar* and *Othello* Off-Broadway and in the Long Wharf Theater stagings of *A Day in the Death of Joe Egg* and *Requiem for a Heavyweight*, as well as starring in the films *The Big Fix* and *Whose Life is It Anyway?* In the late eighties Dreyfuss was featured in films including *Down and Out in Beverly Hills, Stand by Me, Tin Men, Nuts,* and *What about Bob?* He won the Italian Film Journalists Award as Best Actor for *Rosencrantz and Guildenstern are Dead.*

(Opposite) **Richard Dreyfuss as Uncle Louie and Mike Damus as Arty play for matchsticks on the roof of the candy store, built for the film in Ludlow,**

Like millions of Americans in the thirties and forties, Bella found a world of escape, sophistication and romance in the movies. Here Maurice Zuberano's storyboards show the long continuous shot that follows her from her seat at the Bijou up the aisle, through the lobby in a 180-degree circle, to her flirtatious exchange with Johnny.

BELLA
Why not? It's my fourth time. I bet I got the record.

JOHNNY
No. I do. I seen it twelve times.

They both smile. It is clear that Johnny is much like Bella. Very slow and retarded to some degree.

BELLA
I cry at the ending every time. Do you?

JOHNNY
No. I never saw the ending. I always have to start cleaning up.

BELLA
Oh. I'll tell you about it sometime.

JOHNNY
Okay.

Ext. Movie Theater - Night
He nods, then starts to walk away.

BELLA
If you're not gonna be long, I can wait. We could take a walk.

JOHNNY
Yeah, sure. Except I walk the other way.

BELLA
Oh. That's right... Well, I'll see you soon, then... Good night, Johnny.

She smiles, turns and starts to walk away.

JOHNNY
Bella?

BELLA
Yeah?

JOHNNY
You look nice in that dress.

BELLA
Thanks. You look nice in that uniform.

He nods, then turns and goes inside. Bella, feeling good, starts to walk away.

Int. Living Room - Night
Jay and Arty are in the sofa bed. The lamp behind them on the table is lit. They both stare up in the ceiling, wearing pajamas.

JAY
I wish there was a way to get some money to help Pop. I don't mean "kid" money. I mean real money.

ARTY
What if one night we cut off Grandma's braids and sold it to the army for barbed wire.

Jay looks at him as if he's demented.

The upstairs living-room door opens and Bella comes in holding a movie magazine.

BELLA
(crosses to them and whispers) Arty? Jay? Are you asleep?

They look at her.

BELLA
Something wonderful is happening to me except I can't tell you what it is. But you two, you're my good luck charms.

Suddenly Grandma comes out of her room in a long flannel nightgown and wearing her braids long down her back.

GRANDMA
(to Bella) You tink I don't hear you coming up the stairs? You tink I don't know where you've been?

The sequence was filmed with a steadycam—a self-balancing movie camera rigged to be carried and operated by a technician without needing wheels and tracks.

BELLA

Just to the movies, Ma.

GRANDMA

Movies, movies, movies. You waste your life in da movies. Then you throw money away on those movie magazines. You fill your head with dreams that don't happen to people like us.

BELLA

Sometimes they do.

GRANDMA

Never! Never!!... Give me that magazine. I don't want that trash in my house.

BELLA

(embarrassed) Momma, please don't do this to me in front of the boys.

GRANDMA

What do I care what da boys see? Give me that trash, you give it to me. *(she grabs it out of Bella's hand)* When I'm dead you can buy your own magazines.

BELLA

No, I won't. Because when I'm dead you'll still take them away from me.

She runs into her room. Grandma turns her glare on the boys.

GRANDMA

You like to pay my electric bill? Yah?

Jay quickly turns out the light and they both crawl into bed, covers up to their faces. Grandma turns, crosses into her bedroom. In the doorway she stops, turns back and looks at them.

GRANDMA

...You try cutting off my braids, you get your fingers chopped off.

She goes in and slams the door. The boys look at each other.

Ext/Int. Bus on Road - Alabama - Day
Eddie, looking tired, unshaven and pale, tries to write a letter on the rickety bus, packed with servicemen.

EDDIE

"Dear Boys, Somewhere in Alabama, God knows where. Doing pretty good business but had a minor setback last week. The doctor says I have an irregular heartbeat. But, don't worry, I feel fine. And the harder I work now, the quicker we'll all be together. Love, Pop."

Ext. Cemetery - Day
We are focused on three gravestones next to each other, two small ones and a large one. On the two small headstones, we read the names of "Aaron Kurnitz, Age 8"...and "Rose Kurnitz, Age 6"...The large one reads "Carl Kurnitz, Age 42"...

As the camera pulls back, we see Bella with Jay and Arty. Bella puts flowers on the three gravestones.

BELLA

(talking to the gravestone) You know I wouldn't forget your birthday, Aaron. Aaron! These are Eddie's boys, Jay and Arty. They're your nephews, even though they're older than you are...We just came out to say "Happy Birthday, Aaron..." *(she looks at the boys)* You can say it if you want.

JAY

(self-consciously) Happy birthday, Aaron.

ARTY

Yeah. Happy birthday.

BELLA

(to Aaron's grave) I'll see you in September, Rose... So long, Pop. I know we'll finally get to meet some day. I love ya.

She turns and walks away. Arty and Jay follow.

BELLA

(to boys) Thank you for coming. I'm sure Aaron enjoyed it.

JAY

Do you always come here alone?

BELLA

Your Aunt Gert comes sometimes. And your father came once. Grandma never comes. And your Uncle Louie can't.

ARTY

Why not?

BELLA

On account of the work he does.

ARTY

What kind of work?

BELLA

He's a—what do they call it?... He's a bag man.

JAY

What's a bag man?

BELLA

He collects money from people and puts it in this bag. And then gives it to this man who pays him for doing it. *(she looks around, then whispers)* I think he's a gangster.

ARTY

Uncle Louie is?

BELLA

No, no, no. The man he works for... Uncle Louie is just his hunchback.

JAY

His hunchback?

BELLA

Yeah, I think so.

Robert Guy Miranda as Hollywood Harry (so-called for his ties hand-painted with movie stars) lays a one-spot on Jay (Brad Stoll) to tell him when his Uncle Louie shows up.

JAY
Do you mean "henchman"?

BELLA
Yeah, that's it.

ARTY
Does Grandma know?

BELLA
Grandma knows everything. Even about him being a hunchback.

They walk on.

Ext. Street - Candy Store - Day
A few days later. We see a big white convertible sedan slowly come down the street and park in front of the candy store. Two obvious-looking "thugs" are in the car.

Jay is sweeping up outside in front of the store. One of the thugs in the car throws a lit half-cigar at Jay's feet. He is Hollywood Harry, known for his flashy hand-painted ties of movie starlets. Today it's Betty Grable. Jay looks up at him.

HARRY
How's business, kid?

JAY
It's okay.

HARRY
You know Louie Kurnitz?

JAY
Yeah. He's my uncle.

HARRY
Yeah? You see him around?

JAY
No. Not since I've been here.

HARRY
(holds up a dollar bill) Well, when he comes around, you let me know. I got some of these with bigger numbers on it.

He crumples it and throws it at Jay's feet. The car drives off. Jay picks up the dollar and rushes into the store.

Int. Candy Store - Day
Arty is washing off a marble-top table. Two women sit at the other table eating ice cream. Grandma sits behind the open cash register counting her cash. Jay comes in and crosses to Arty.

JAY
(voice low) Some guys were here looking for Uncle Louie. They gave me a dollar.

ARTY
I get half, right?

JAY
They look like killers to me. I wonder what they want?

GRANDMA
(looks up) You two want to talk, you sit down and buy someting. Don't annoy my customers.

She bangs the register shut.

JAY
I was just going.

GRANDMA
Ya, ya.

ARTY
(aside to him) I wonder what those guys would give us for Grandma?

They go back to work.

Ext. The Hudson River - Day
Bella is walking along the banks of the river with Johnny. He is wearing a suit and bow tie. Nothing fits him too well. He looks a little downcast.

BELLA
I can't stay here long, Johnny. Momma would never believe it if I told her I got lost going to the bank.

JOHNNY
(looks at ground) That's okay.

BELLA
You, you look a little sad. Is anything wrong?

JOHNNY
No.

BELLA
Yes, it is. I can see it in your eyes. You can tell me. I'm your friend Bella.

JOHNNY
I know who you are.

BELLA
I know that you know. So why can't you tell me?

JOHNNY
(looks up at the sky) ...I want to join the army.

BELLA
The army? Our army?

JOHNNY
Yeah. But they wouldn't take me. I couldn't pass the—the—whatever they give you, I couldn't pass it.

BELLA
Well, I'm kinda glad.

JOHNNY
You are?

Jay (Brad Stoll) **watches the gangsters drive away.**

BELLA

Sure. Because if you were in the army, I would miss you.

JOHNNY

I would miss you too.

BELLA

Well, good. Cause now we won't have to miss each other because we'll be together.

JOHNNY

Yeah... I'm not gonna be an usher all my life.

BELLA

Yeah, I know. You told me.

They walk

BELLA

(Bella moves closer to him) Do you know what color my eyes are, Johnny?

JOHNNY

No. What?

BELLA

You're looking right at them.

JOHNNY

(squints) Oh...I'm a little color-blind.

BELLA

You have beautiful eyes.

JOHNNY

Nahh. Men don't have beautiful eyes.

BELLA

Oh, they do. Don't tell me. *(she moves very close)* Do you wanna kiss me?

JOHNNY

(he turns his head away) ...Yeah... Yeah, I do. I really would.

BELLA

Well, then kiss me.

JOHNNY

(he looks the other way) ...I will.

BELLA

I mean now. Today. Sometime today... We've done it before, you know. Are you gonna put your arms around me or not?

JOHNNY

Don't tell me how to do it. I know how to do it.

BELLA

Then do it. Don't say you're gonna do it.

JOHNNY

I said okay.

Johnny (David Strathairn) **confesses to Bella** (Mercedes Ruehl) **he was turned down by the army, as they walk along the banks of the Hudson (actually the Ohio River).**

Johnny and Bella play out a film fantasy—and still photographer Zade Rosenthal makes it look like the Burt Lancaster and Deborah Kerr clinch in *From Here to Eternity*.

He grabs her and kisses her on the lips, first gently... then warmly, then passionately... It lingers...then he presses harder and pulls her to him... And kisses even harder.

BELLA

(trying to speak) Okay, that's enough. *(he's still kissing her)* Johnny!... I can't breathe, Johnny... Okay, that's enough for today. *(He presses forward one more time, kissing her harder, then he lets go... She looks at him, gasping.)*

BELLA

I don't know why they didn't take you in the army.

Ext. Backyard of House - Close-up - Jay's Face - Day

JAY

Married? You're getting married?

Pull back.

Bella is hanging the laundry on a line. Arty is carrying the wicker basket and Jay is handing her each piece.

BELLA

Not so loud. Grandma'll hear you. Why do you think I'm telling you out here?

She looks up to window. There is no one there.

JAY

(lower) You're getting married?

She nods.

ARTY

Have you found anyone yet?

BELLA

What do you mean have I found anyone yet? Of course I found someone. His name is Johnny. He's an usher at the Bijou. Jay! Arty! I've never been so happy in all my life.

She keeps glancing up at the window.

ARTY

How come he's not in the army?

BELLA

(as she hangs pieces) Oh, he wanted to go, but they wouldn't take him on the account he's handicap.

JAY

What handicap?

BELLA

He's got a reading handicap.

ARTY

You mean he has bad eyes?

BELLA

No, no, no. He just has trouble learning things. The way I did. He even went to a special school for a while. He was in the Home once. Yeah, the one that Grandma's always telling me I'm going to go to if I'm not a good girl.

Int. Grandma's Room - Day
She peers out the window. We see Bella and the boys down in the yard. The clouds roll in and we see lightning and hear a rumble of thunder in the distance.

Ext. Backyard - Day

JAY

Well, how old is he?

BELLA

He's thirty. Maybe forty. But he is so handsome. And, um, he doesn't want to be an usher forever either. He wants to open up his own restaurant... with me. I would be the cook and he would be the manager.

JAY

Could he do that? Manage a restaurant if he couldn't read the menus?

BELLA

Oh, I would help him out with all of that. But see, the only thing is, he doesn't make a lot of money and we'd need about five thousand dollars to open a restaurant. And I don't know if Grandma would give it to me. Do you?

ARTY

I don't think she's gonna let you go to the movies much anymore.

JAY

Your mother has five thousand dollars?

BELLA

Shhh, she has more than that. She's got ten or fifteen thousand dollars. I'm not supposed to tell anyone.

JAY

Where does she keep it? In the bank?

BELLA.

No, no, no. She keeps in right here in the house somewhere. She changes the hiding place every year. Not even Gert or Louie or your father knows where it is... There! We got all the laundry up.

And suddenly it starts to pour. Heavily.

BELLA

Oh oh.

She looks up to the window.

Ext. Backyard - Grandma's Window - Day
She looks down at Bella in the rain.

GRANDMA

(half to herself) Dumkopf! Stupid dumkopf!

She slams the window down.

Ext. Backyard - Porch - Bella and the Boys - Day
They run in and get onto the porch out of the rain. They are all soaking wet.

BELLA
This always happens to me.

JAY
Fifteen thousand dollars. That's a lot of money.

BELLA
Oh, Jay, promise me you won't tell Grandma that I told you, Jay.

JAY
I promise.

BELLA
Arty?

ARTY
She and I have very short conversations.

BELLA
I know I can trust you boys. *(she starts inside with wicker basket)* Oh, you know what? I thought of a name for the restaurant... "La Bella Johnny."

JAY
That's nice.

BELLA
Yeah. I just hope he can read it.

She goes inside. The boys look at the rain.

ARTY
Wait'll Grandma meets Johnny. He'll be back in the Home in a week.

Int. Living Room - Night
Arty is in bed, the lamp is still on. Jay looks around the room.

JAY
Where would someone like Grandma hide her money?

ARTY
You're not thinking of stealing it, are you?

JAY
(still looking) No. But what if we just borrowed it? I would just love to send Pop an envelope with nine thousand dollars in it.

ARTY
Who would he think sent it to him? God?

JAY
No. He had an uncle in Poland who died. We could say he left the money in his will to Pop.

ARTY
Jay, do you think the Germans would let some Jew in Poland send nine thousand dollars to some Jew in Alabama?

Montage of Jay searching

JAY (V.O.)
...I searched the house whenever Grandma was out.

Int. Kitchen - Day

Int. Grandma's Room - Day
Jay checks Grandma's closet when suddenly the shadow of a figure with a cane appears. Jay sees it and falls to the floor in fear. It is only Arty with Grandma's cane.

Ext. House - Night
We see the lights of the house go out.

JAY (V.O.)
...And then I thought, "hey! The candy store!!"

Int. Candy Store - Night
We see Jay and Arty coming down the stairs in their pajamas. Jay carries a flashlight.

JAY
You look under the candy counter. I'll look under the ice-cream cartons.

ARTY
Get me a chocolate cone while you're at it. With sprinkles.

JAY
Shut up, will ya?

As they look, we suddenly hear a man's voice in the dark.

MAN
That's breakin and enterin', kid. Two to five years for both of you.

JAY
Who's that?

He swings the flashlight around the room and there, sitting at a table against the wall, is a man in a suit, a hat and a black bag on the table. He shields his face. He is in his late thirties.

MAN
Hey, get that outa my face, will ya?

Jay shuts off the light.

JAY
What you want, mister? There's nothing to steal in here.

MAN
Is that you, Jay?

JAY
Yeah.

MAN
And Arty?

ARTY
Yeah. Who are you?

The man steps out of the dark into a shaft of light coming from the outside street lamp.

MAN (LOUIE)
It's your Uncle Louie! Whaddya know? A couple of big guys now, ain't you?

JAY
You been sitting here long?

LOUIE
Yeah, since Ma closed up the store. I was waitin' for her to go to sleep.

JAY
Nobody told us you were coming tonight.

LOUIE
Nobody knew. It was a surprise even for me. Come here. Come on. Give me a hug... You heard me, move it!

They both move to him quickly, he puts an arm around each of their shoulders and hugs them. He chuckles.

LOUIE
A couple a' middle-weights here.

He picks up the black satchel and starts for the stairs.

JAY
Are you staying tonight?

Louie, on the stairs, as they follow him:

LOUIE
Yeah, yeah. A couple a' days, maybe a week. They're paintin' my apartment.

ARTY
You didn't know they were going to paint your apartment?

LOUIE
They just found the right color paint tonight. Hard to find with the war on.

He opens the upstairs door and goes into the apartment.

Int. Grandma's Room - Night
She's in bed. She hears Louie's voice in the other room. She makes a disgruntled sound, then turns over in her bed.

Int. Living Room - Night
Louie turns lamp on. The two boys are on the bed, Louie has taken off his hat and is undoing his tie. The black satchel is on a table close to Louie.

LOUIE
...Your Pop and me used to do the same thing when we was kids. We never took anything during the day. No candy, no ice cream. But as soon as Ma let her braids down and turned out the lights, we was down there lappin' up the cream like a couple a' cats.

A stranger in the candy store catches the boys (Brad Stoll and Mike Damus) **searching for Grandma's hidden cash.**

He takes off his coat. We see he has a gun in a shoulder holster. The boys' eyes widen at it as Louie keeps talking.

LOUIE
The fun was outsmartin' Ma 'cause she was quick. She could tell if there was salt missing from a pretzel...so the next morning at breakfast, she'd just stare at me, right into my eyeballs, pupil to pupil, never blinkin'... Her eyes looked like two district attorneys... But I'd just stare right back at her until she'd look away from me, down for the count... Yeah, me and Ma used to love to put on the gloves and go the distance....

They still stare at him.

LOUIE
What is it? *(he looks at gun)* This? *(he takes it out)* Don't worry about it. I'm holdin' it for a friend. This cop I know is on a camping trip with his kids. He don't want no accidents.

He puts the gun under his pants belt, just over the fly. He winks at them.

It's Louie (Richard Dreyfuss), Grandma's toughest son, who will be the real thief in the story but also a hero to Jay and Arty.

JAY
Is it loaded?

LOUIE
(looks down at gun) Gee, I hope not. If it goes off now, I'd have to become a ballerina.

He takes holster off and puts it and gun behind him on the table. He starts to unzip his pants.

JAY
You know, I never knew a policeman could lend his gun to somebody.

LOUIE
(a grim look) You got a real smart brother there, did you know that, Arty? You're right, Jay. It's my gun. I'm a bodyguard for a very important, very prominent political figure. It's kind of like being an FBI man, only they call it something else.

He takes off his pants.

ARTY
You mean a henchman?

LOUIE
(glares at him) Who's been telling you stories like that? Jay?

ARTY
No. I swear.

LOUIE
Don't you ever repeat that word around to anyone again, you understand me?

ARTY
I didn't mean to say it. I was thinking of hunchback.

LOUIE
A couple of jokers here, huh? Don't pull my leg, Arty. It might come off in your hands.

Louie hangs his pants neatly over the back of the chair.

Okay, now let's discuss a little business here. I'll tell you what. Why don't you come and work for me? Five dollars a week split between youse, cash on the barrel. Whaddya say?

JAY/ARTY
Sure.

LOUIE
There's your first week's pay, boys.

ARTY
Where?

LOUIE
Where? Where? In Jay's pocket, that's where. Go ahead and look, Arty.

Arty looks in Jay's pajama pocket. He takes out a bill.

ARTY

A five dollar bill. How'd you do that?

LOUIE

These hands was touched by genius. I could have been a concert violinist, but the handkerchief kept fallin' off my neck.

ARTY

What?

LOUIE

Too fast for you, huh, boys? Never mind. Okay, so Arty, do you think you can drive a car?

ARTY

I'm only thirteen years old... I'm a pretty good roller skater.

LOUIE

You are? That's good, because I'm spinnin' your wheels, kid. *(snaps fingers)* Hey, c'mon, wake up and live, c'mon, it's a fast world out there. Jeezes.

He continues getting undressed.

JAY

What would we have to do for the money?

LOUIE

Nothin'. Like if someone comes around here lookin' for me, you don't know nothin' and you ain't seen nothin'.

ARTY

There were two men here the other day looking for you.

LOUIE

Oh, yeah? What'd they look like?

ARTY

One had a broken nose and he was wearing—

LOUIE

Wearing a Betty Grable tie. That's, uh, that's Hollywood Harry and his brother. Okay. So if they show up here again askin' questions, what do you say to 'em?

ARTY/JAY

Nothing!

LOUIE

Smart boys. Jay, look in Arty's pocket.

He looks in Jay's pajama pocket and pulls out a bill.

JAY

Another five dollars

LOUIE

I could have played Carnegie Hall.

JAY

We wouldn't be doing anything wrong, would we?

LOUIE

Hey, you're my brother's kids. Do you think I'd get you involved with something stupid? Don't be stupid. *(he starts for the bathroom)* C'mon, it's late. I'm gonna wash up.

LOUIE

Oh. One more thing. *(he crosses back and points to black satchel)* Don't touch that. You see, uh, it's got my valuables in it. You know, my driver's license and my draft card and, my uh, my new cuff links. Alright, forget about it. Never mind.... I'll just put it somewhere else so you won't have to worry about it.

He picks up the bag and heads to the bathroom with it.

LOUIE

Oh, Arty! See if there's anything else in your pajama bottoms.

Arty looks inside his pajama bottoms, feels around.

ARTY

There's nothing in there.

LOUIE

Yeah, well, don't worry about it, kid. You're young yet.

He chuckles, goes to the bathroom and closes the door. Jay and Arty look at each other.

Lying low at Grandma's, Richard Dreyfuss as Louie beds down with Arty and Jay (Mike Damus and Brad Stoll)**. His sleeping with his gun gives them a sleepless night.**

ARTY

He's incredible. It's like having a James Cagney movie in your own house.

Int. Bella's Bedroom - Night
Bella's in bed, sleeping. We are in fairly tight on her. Suddenly we hear Louie's voice whisper in the dark.

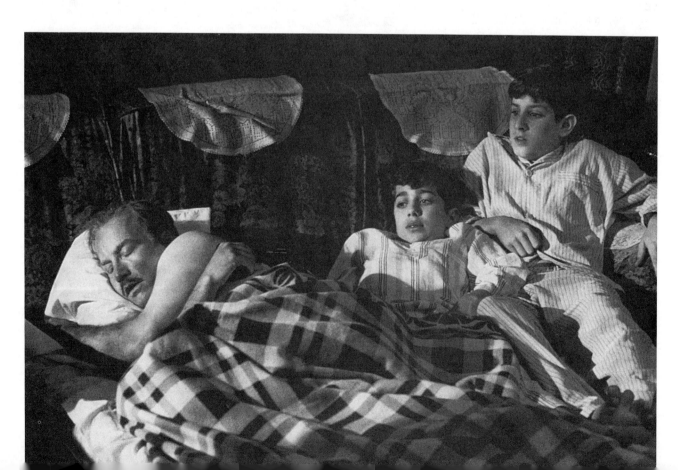

LOUIE
How you doin', Princess?

Bella wakes up, startled.

BELLA
Louie! Louie! *(they hug)* You're in trouble, I know it. Whenever you come at night, you're in trouble.

LOUIE
I got you to protect me, don't I?

BELLA
Me?... You'd be better off with a big dog, Louie.

They laugh and hug again.

Int. Bedroom - Night
Louie, in Grandma's bathrobe, comes in the darkened room. The boys are in bed, but not asleep. Louie sits on the edge of the bed, holds up his gun, flips open the chamber to see if bullets are in, they are, cocks the gun, puts it under pillow and goes to bed. The boys, petrified, lean away as far as possible on their side of the bed, scared stiff.

Int. Candy Store - Day
It's the next day. Two customers are seated at the fountain. Bella is making them ice-cream sodas. Grandma is behind the cash register going over the books. Two small kids are looking at comic books from the rack on the wall. Arty and Jay are cleaning up around the store. Suddenly, Grandma grabs one of the two kids on the way out of the store.

GRANDMA
You were reading or you were stealing from me?

1ST KID
We were just looking, that's all.

GRANDMA
Uh, heh? And vot's dis?

She reaches inside his sweater and pulls out a comic book.

GRANDMA
You know what happens to people who steal from me?

She whacks him on the head with her open hand. It's loud and hard. The kid yells in pain.

GRANDMA
Next time I call da police.

She whacks him in the head with the magazine. The two kids start out the store.

1ST KID
(in tears) You dirty Kraut!

They run off.

Arty and Jay at the table

They've been watching.

ARTY

I don't think we should look for her money anymore.

Grandma starts up the stairs.

GRANDMA

Yakob! Go outside and pull down da awning. Artur! Go down in da cellar and bring up da bottles of syrup. I don't feed you for not working.

She goes up and inside. They all look at her. Bella crosses to them.

BELLA

Jay, Arty! Have you two thought of anything yet? About how I could tell Grandma about me and you-know-who?

JAY

Gee, we've been kinda busy ourselves.

BELLA

Okay, sure. I understand. If you do think of something, I'm going to give you each a dollar. I know you can use that.

She crosses back to the counter.

JAY

(to Arty) You know we could make a great living just from this family.

Int. Upstairs Bathroom - Day
Louie is in bathroom, shaving. The door opens slightly and Grandma stands there. She looks at the black satchel on the sink.

LOUIE

(smiles) Hey, Ma! Happy to see me?

GRANDMA

How long you staying?

LOUIE

(smiles) That's what I love. A warm welcome... I don't know. A couple of days. Maybe a week.

GRANDMA

(looks at bag again) Maybe a couple of days is better.

She turns and walks away. Louie leans out and calls after her.

LOUIE

I love you, too, Ma.

Ext. Store - Day
Jay is letting down the awning. The big white car pulls up in front of the store. Hollywood Harry and his brother.

HARRY

Hey, kid. Come here. C'here. Come over here.

Jay looks at him nervously, then crosses to the car. He holds up a five dollar bill.

Bella (Mercedes Ruehl) **asks Jay and Arty** (Brad Stoll and Mike Damus) **to help her tell Grandma about her boyfriend Johnny.**

To send a message to Louie, Robert Guy Miranda as Hollywood Harry stuffs a fiver into Jay's pocket. But Jay (Brad Stoll) **will throw it back.**

HARRY
You know what this is?

JAY
Sure. It's a five dollar bill.

Harry puts it in Jay's shirt.

HARRY
You tell Uncle Louie that Friday night the dance is over.

JAY
I haven't seen him. I don't want your money.

He takes the bill out of his pocket and gives it back to Harry.

HARRY
Good. Then you tell him for free.

The car drives off. Jay watches them go.

Int. The Cellar - Day
Arty starts to pick up the large bottle of chocolate syrup. Suddenly, he spies a box of Oh, Henry candy bars. He looks around, opens it, takes a few bars out and puts them in his pocket. He opens one and takes a bite out of it. He puts the box back in its place. He chews quickly, then takes another bite, and we suddenly hear a crunch and he grabs his mouth in pain.

ARTY
Oh! Oh God! My tooth!

It's raining. Grandma, with her hat on, is half-dragging Arty down the street. He is holding his aching tooth.

ARTY
I just took one little bite. I don't need a dentist.

GRANDMA
You eat my candy, you go see my dentist. Here we go. Quick, quick, open ze door. Quick.

Int. Dining Room - Dusk
Arty holds his aching jaw in pain. (While he stirs his soup aimlessly)

ARTY
...He didn't even give me any gas for the pain.

LOUIE
You're lucky. When we was kids, we couldn't afford no dentist. Ma pulled my back molars out with an open Coke bottle.

The boys are shocked. They look at Bella. Bella looks at them and shrugs, not remembering that incident. Like "who knows, maybe she did."

Grandma comes in from the kitchen with a plate of vegetables. She puts them down, sits, looks at Arty.

GRANDMA
You sit here all night till you finish that soup.

ARTY

I tried. I can't get it down. It's awful.

GRANDMA

You eat it up quick, you don't taste it.

ARTY

(under his breath) I would taste this if I didn't have a tongue.

Louie smiles and looks away. Bella looks shocked, sensing trouble.

GRANDMA

You don't vant a tongue, I can arrange that too.

JAY

Maybe if he just had some plain hot tea, Grandma.

GRANDMA

(to Jay) Did I ask you? Maybe instead of your dinner, you go down and count da pretzels.

JAY

What pretzels?

GRANDMA

(cutting bread) In da pretzel jar. There were nine pretzels in da jar dis morning und only six tonight. We don't sell no pretzels today. You let someone steal pretzels, you pay for it.

JAY

What??

This also amuses Louie.

GRANDMA

Don't "what" me. You don't "what" Grandma. Go help Bella wash up the dishes and den you clean up da basement.

JAY

I'm not through eating yet.

GRANDMA

...Bella, take his plate.

BELLA

(pleadingly) Aw, Ma.

GRANDMA

(to Bella) Take-his-plate!

Bella thinks about it, then takes Jay's plate. Then as she passes behind Grandma, she looks at Jay and mouths the words "I'll save it for you." She points to the plate, then at the kitchen. Grandma turns and looks at her. Bella gives her a smile and goes.

Louie smiles.

GRANDMA

You find this funny, Louie?

LOUIE
(smiles) Don't try takin' my plate, Ma. Louie's hungry.

He winks at Arty, and continues eating as he looks at Grandma, knowing he's taken her on and won.

INT. KITCHEN - DUSK
Bella is at the sink, washing the dishes. Jay's plate is on the table. Jay comes in.

BELLA
Eat it quick. And no noise.

Jay quickly goes to his plate and gobbles it down as fast as he can.

BELLA
Talked to Gert. She's coming over tomorrow night. That's when I'm going to tell Grandma, okay? I need you and Arty. You gonna back me up on this, aren't you?

Jay nods as he tries to finish his food. Bella bites off a piece of bread.

BELLA
And don't get Grandma upset 'cause I really need her in a good mood. Look at me, I can't stop eating. I ate three pretzels today and I never eat pretzels.

JAY
You ate the pretzels?... Then why didn't you tell her at the table?

BELLA
Oh, she knew I ate the pretzels. She even said to me, "Why are you eating so much? You nervous about something?"... Of course I'm nervous about something.

The pressure is on Louie (Richard Dreyfuss)**: his gangster pals are still parked outside and he hasn't handed over the cash he owes them.**

He nods and hands her his plate. She takes it, turns and drops it.

The dish smashes as Grandma walks in and looks down at the plate.

BELLA
I'm sorry, Momma. It was an accident. I'll pay for it.

JAY
(to Grandma) No, no. Put it on my bill with my pretzels.

Grandma glares at him.

Ext. Street - Night
We see Hollywood Harry's car slowly drive by.

Int. Living Room - Night

LOUIE
Just wastin' gas, boys.

ARTY
Huh?

LOUIE
Ah, nothin', nothin'! It's Hollywood Harry. Tryin' to shake Louie outta the tree.

Arty jumps out of bed and rushes to the window. He looks around and sees the car.

LOUIE
Heh, heh, heh.

ARTY
Oh, I forgot. They told Jay to tell you that Friday night the dance is over.

LOUIE
(smiles) Oh, yeah? Don't worry about it. Uncle Louie can outdance a couple a Bronx palookas like that any day.

He walks away from the window.

ARTY
I wish I was as tough as you!

LOUIE
Well, you're gettin' there, Arty. You took on the old lady tonight.
That took moxie.

ARTY
What's moxie?

LOUIE
What's moxie?

Louie looks at him. Thinks, then plants his feet apart, takes a defiant position, extends his arms with his hands in front of him, then beckons with curled up fingers as if to say, "Come on, tough guy. I'm waitin' for you."

LOUIE
That's moxie.

He winks at Arty and heads for the bathroom.

ARTY
Uncle Louie. Are you in trouble?

LOUIE
I was never not in trouble.

He goes to the bathroom.

Ext. Street - Night
The car is now parked out there in front of the store.

Int. Living Room - Night
Arty is at the window in his pajamas. He points his finger out the window towards the street, like a gun.

ARTY
Hey, Hollywood Harry. Take this right through your Betty Grable tie.

He shoots four times, makes the gunshot noise himself. Then he "takes a slug" in the heart.

ARTY
Agghh! you no good dirty little kid killer.

He drops to the floor, prone, as Jay comes in the door looking exhausted.

JAY
Well, that store doesn't have to be cleaned for a year now. Hey, guess what Uncle Louie came down and gave me?

ARTY
I don't know. I'm dead.

JAY
(showing him) A dollar. You want to go to the movies on Sunday?

ARTY
(jumps up) Movies?? *(he rushes over to Grandma's chair and starts jumping up and down on it)* Let's go to a war movie and see them kill German Grandmas. Yah Yah Yah Yah!!

He keeps jumping up and down as Grandma appears in her doorway with her cane and braids down. He stops, panicked.

GRANDMA
Vot do you tink you're doing?

ARTY
Dusting your chair?

GRANDMA
Nein! I don't think so... From now on, Artur, I don't think I'll be so nice to you.

She turns and goes.

Int. Bella's Bedroom - Night
She is in her bed, the room is dark. She is looking out towards the sky, up to the shining stars above.

BELLA
Star light, Star bright, first star I see tonight...wish I may, I wish I might... I forget the rest but please help me tomorrow night.

Somewhere in the South. Eddie sits on a step of the rooming house, reading a letter amidst the sounds of summer insects.

JAY(V.O.)
...That same night, Uncle Louie decided to take me and Arty swimming down at the river, knowing that Hollywood Harry was outside waiting for him... I don't think he really wanted to go swimming. He just wanted to show them how tough he was.

Int. Cellar
Louie, Jay and Arty come down the cellar steps. They are dressed.

LOUIE
I'll show you where I used to sneak out when I was a kid. Yeah, I was really hot to see my girl friend, Francie, but Ma didn't like her.

JAY
Why not?

LOUIE
Ah, 'cause Francie was married and I was thirteen and a half. Come here...come here...

He starts to slide away a table that sits against the back wall. Louie signals to them to help him. They move the table. There is a heavy board against the wall. Louie moves that away, revealing a crawl space that leads away from the house.

Uncle Louie (Richard Dreyfuss) **shows Jay and Arty the tunnel that he and Bella dug when they were kids. Tonight uncle and nephews will slip through the mobsters' surveillance and go for a swim.**

LOUIE

Twenty-two feet. Me and Bella, we dug it ourselves.

ARTY

Bella did?

LOUIE

Yeah. I told her China was on the other side. She got all excited 'cause she loves Chinese food.

Int. Crawl Space - Night
Louie is in the lead, Jay and Arty behind him.

JAY

(as they crawl) Did Grandma ever know about this?

LOUIE

Yes, she found out after a while. I crawled out the other side and she was waiting for me and, whacko, I got that big German hand across the head. And then it was prison for me.

ARTY

What prison?

LOUIE

Grandma's closet. She'd lock me in there for two, three hours at a time. No light, no water, no food, just enough air to breathe.

JAY

That would make me crazy.

LOUIE

Tough as nails.

Int. Grandma's Bedroom - Night

Ext. Next Door - Yard - Night
There is a manhole cover in the pathway. It suddenly lifts up and slides over as Louie crawls out, looks around and helps Jay and Arty out.

LOUIE

C'mon, c'mon. Arty, c'mon.

JAY

Funny place for a manhole cover.

LOUIE

(slides cover back on) I stole it from down the street. Me and Bella did. I told her it was to keep everyone from China from movin' into our house.

He crawls along the ground to the fence, then creeps up and peers into it. The boys follow.

On the other side of the fence, we see the candy store and across the street from it, we see the big sedan still ominously parked with Hollywood Harry and his crony sitting there.

Ext. The River - Night
Arty and Jay are in the water, everything off but their shorts. Louie stands on the shore, backs up.

LOUIE

Alright. Back up, boys! Back up, c'mon. Outta the way! Outta the way! Here comes Louie Kurnitz, King of Yonkers.

He makes a long run and jumps high into the water. He comes up for air.

LOUIE

Okay, what did I just do?

ARTY

...You jumped in the water.

LOUIE

No, you stupid jerk. I made a splash. That's what life's all about. Makin' a big splash... Otherwise you die a nobody. And I ain't dyin' till I'm somebody.

He splashes water at the boys and they join in the water fight. The first fun they've had in a month.

The Edge of the River - Night
They're huddled around a small fire, drying out their clothes. Louie smokes a cigarette. He gives Arty one from his pack.

JAY

...Did Grandma ever put my father in the closet?

LOUIE

Not a chance. She used to open the closet door and he'd tie himself to the radiator. Even if it was hot. No, Eddie was afraid of her... Now Aunt Gert, she really was more afraid that your old man. She used to talk in her sleep, you know. One night Ma heard her sayin' some things she didn't like. So Gert didn't get no supper for a week. Until she learned to sleep holdin' her breath. Which is why she talks so funny today.

Ext. The Roadway - Night
Now with their clothes on, the three of them are walking down the road back to Yonkers.

JAY

Did you ever want to run away?

LOUIE

You kidding? I did. Twelve times.

ARTY

Twelve times?

LOUIE

Yeah, still a record in Yonkers. The last time she wouldn't take me back. She told the policeman she didn't know me.

JAY

Did you hate her for that?

LOUIE

Yeah. Sure, I hated her plenty... Till one day I realized I could survive without her or anybody else. Hell of a teacher Ma was.

Jay and Arty look at each other. Louis puts his arms around each boy, holding them as they walk.

LOUIE
So whaddya think of your Uncle Louie, boys? You like him?

ARTY
(smiles) Yeah.

JAY
You bet.

LOUIE
Don't get to used to it. Once you start dependin' on people, you'll never make it on your own.

He moves off ahead of them, trotting and shadow-boxing like a prize-fighter in training.

LOUIE
Understand? Understand? C'mon, c'mon, c'mon, c'mon.

Int. Candy Store - Morning
Arty comes in from outside with a broom.

BELLA
Oh, Arty!

She takes her apron off.

BELLA
Would you watch the store for awhile until Grandma comes down? I have to do some shopping for tonight's dinner.

ARTY
But I can't make any ice-cream sodas or anything. Maybe a glass of water, that's all.

BELLA
Grandma'll be right down. *(she takes her purse)* And, Arty, don't forget. You and Jay promised you would back me up tonight.

She shakes Arty's hand and goes. Arty goes behind the counter. The cops look at him. Arty's head is barely over the counter.

COP
(to Arty) How you doing, son?

ARTY
Okay... Would you like a glass of water?

Suddenly Hollywood Harry enters. We see his big white sedan parked outside the store with his brother at the wheel. Harry crosses to the counter. Arty looks panicked.

COP
(to Harry) Morning.

HARRY
You bet.

COP
I wouldn't leave that car there too long. Pretty close to the hydrant.

Robert Guy Miranda as Hollywood Harry sports his signature handpainted tie and Panama hat. "When a man wore a mustache in the forties," says chief makeup artist Dan Striepeke, "it had a very tailored look, almost a little vanity piece—like William Powell in *The Thin Man.*"

HARRY

(smiles) Be gone in a minute. *(to Arty)* Hey, big guy. How about a cup of coffee. It's right behind you.

Arty turns, sees the coffee in the percolator, pours some into a cup and puts it on the counter.

HARRY

No, no, no. I wanted to take it with me.

ARTY

You can take it. Just bring back the cup.

The cops smile, put down their money and leave. Harry watches them go, then to Arty:

HARRY

You boys enjoy your little swim last night?

ARTY

Huh?

HARRY

Louie knows we ain't gonna make a move unless he's got the little black bag with him.

The upstairs door opens and Grandma comes out. She sees Harry. He sees her. She's seen him before. He tips the brim of his hat and smiles. Then he throws a dollar on the counter.

HARRY

(to Arty) But he'll have it with him tonight. You can bet his life on it.

He winks at Arty and goes. Arty picks up the money and looks at Grandma.

Int. Thrift Shop - Day
Secondhand dresses and marked-down rejects. Bella is looking through the dresses.

Bella continues to look as she suddenly sees a woman about twenty-four, with an eight-month old baby in her arms, and pushing an empty stroller, as she looks through dresses.

BELLA

Teresa? Is that you?... It's Bella...

TERESA

Bella! Hello!

BELLA

Oh, my God! Is that yours? You were just a baby yourself a few years ago... Is he a boy or a girl?

TERESA

Boy... Andrew... Looks like his father, I think.

BELLA

Really, your husband looks like this? He must be very cute. I used to make ice-cream cones for your mother. *(to Teresa)* You think I could hold him a second?

TERESA

(hesitant, then relents) Alright. But be careful. He squirms a lot.

BELLA

Don't worry. A baby is one thing I'd never drop.

She takes the baby, holds him and rocks him. To baby:

BELLA

You are so cute.

We hear the baby giggle. Bella beams.

BELLA

He likes me. All babies like me.

She hugs him.

Ext. Street - Day
Hollywood and his brother sit in the sedan watching the store.

Ext. Rooftop of House - Day
Louie and Arty are sitting on the tarred ground of the roof of the house. It is sunny and Louie is in his undershirt, smoking a cigarette. They are playing poker, betting matchsticks.

LOUIE

Alright. I see your raise and raise you five more sticks.

He throws in sticks.

ARTY

(holding cards) And what do I do?

LOUIE

It depends on what's in your hand, Dumbo.

ARTY

(tips cards) You want to see?

LOUIE

No, I don't wanna. *(takes Arty's sticks and throws them in the pot)* You call me... What have you got?

ARTY

Four cards. Is that any good?

LOUIE

Yeah. If I was a blind man. *(throws him another card)* Here. Now what do you got?

ARTY

I got five cards.

LOUIE

(clenching his teeth) I know you've got five cards. I just gave you five cards. Don't get me crazy, kid. I'm not in the mood... Just declare.

ARTY

Can't I bet first?

"All babies like me," says Bella (Mercedes Ruehl), **who at thirty-six craves a family of her own.**

LOUIE
We already bet!! We bet and we raised. Then we re-raised the raise... Alright. You wanna bet, bet. What do you bet?

ARTY
I think I'll bluff.

LOUIE
You're gonna bluff? You're telling me you're gonna bluff? If you tell me you're bluffing, then I know you're bluffing. Then I already win.

ARTY
Why? Maybe I'm just bluffing that I'm bluffing.

LOUIE
(grabs Arty's cards) Gimme the cards. *(slams them down)* Get away from me. You play like your old man. Like a loser. You wanna end up selling scrap iron like him?

ARTY
No. *(he looks at his cards and shows Louie)* I've got four aces. Does that lose?

LOUIE
(looks) ...Yeah. Yeah, that loses. Four aces stink.

ARTY
Why?

LOUIE
Because that's the name of this game...four aces stink. Take another look.

Arty gets up and peers cautiously over the roof ledge and looks down.

Ext. The Street. - Day
We see the top of the big white sedan parked across from the store.

The Roof - Day
Arty gets down and turns to Louie.

ARTY
They're still there...so I guess you're not going to leave tonight.

LOUIE
Don't bet on it, Arty. That's one game I got you beat.

97

Uncle Louie (Richard Dreyfuss) **tells Arty** (Mike Damus) **about betting, bluffing and Grandma.**

Louie is sitting on the ground, his back to the wall in the shade. He drinks a bottle of Coke and hands one to Arty, who sits next to him.

ARTY
Poker and Coca-Cola. If Grandma knew, she'd throw me off the roof.

LOUIE
You don't think much of her, so you?

ARTY
She's so mean.

LOUIE
(he drinks some Coke) When she was twelve years old, her old man takes her to a political rally in Berlin. The cops break it up with sticks on horseback. Somebody throws a rock, and a cop bashes in her old man's head, and then a horse goes down and crushes Ma's foot. And nobody ever fixed it. Hurts every single day of her life. I never once seen her take even an aspirin. That's moxie, kid.

Int. Living Room - Day
Arty is at the table, writing a letter. Jay walks in, excitedly.

JAY
Where's Uncle Louie?

ARTY
Taking a shower...

JAY
I have to talk to him.

ARTY
About what?

JAY
It's private business.

ARTY

You don't have any private business. All you got is a job that costs you twelve cents a day.

JAY

Not for long. I'm going to ask Uncle Louie to take me with him tonight.

ARTY

What?

JAY

I want to make some money. Get a job somewhere. If we wait for Pop to come home, I'll owe Grandma more than Pop owes the loan shark.

ARTY

Well, take me with you.

JAY

Take you??? You're only a kid. Besides, she doesn't treat you the way she treats me.

ARTY

I'm afraid of her, Jay. A horse fell on her when she was a kid and she hasn't taken an aspirin yet.

Ext. Johnny's House - Day
It's a tiny house in a poor neighborhood. An elderly couple sits on a porch, the father reading a newspaper. Bella and Johnny stand under a tree, not near but within sight of the older couple. Johnny keeps glancing back at them, nervously.

BELLA

I had my hair done. Did you notice?

JOHNNY

Oh, yeah... It looks the same to me.

BELLA

It is. I told them, "Don't do it any different because my friend might not like it."

She laughs. Johnny looks back at his parents.

BELLA

So do you think I could...meet your parents today?

JOHNNY

Oh. Oh...well...it's just not a good day today.

BELLA

Why is that?

JOHNNY

I could just tell.

BELLA

Okay... Nothing's wrong, is it?

JOHNNY

Oh.

Mike Damus as Arty. The child actor understudied this role in the Broadway play, but only performed once. This is his film debut.

BELLA
Everything is still on.

JOHNNY
Yeah, sure... It's just not a good day today.

He glances back at them.

BELLA
Well, I'd better get started. Tonight's the big dinner. Wish me luck, Johnny.

He nods, arms folded, looking down.

BELLA
Okay. That's enough for me.

She turns to go and gives a little smile and nod to his parents.

Int. Living Room - Day
Jay and Arty on the sofa. Louie, with a towel around his neck, is combing his hair in the mirror. A clean shirt across a chair.

LOUIE
(laughs) You want to go with me?... Why? It's cold out there, Jay. It's dangerous out there.

JAY
I know. But there's money out there.

Louie starts to put on his shirt.

LOUIE
Oh, I see. You're looking to get rich fast.

JAY
No. Not for me. To give to Pop.

LOUIE
Ain't that nice. Like Robin Hood.

JAY
I don't want to rob people.

LOUIE
No? Who do you want to rob?

JAY
No one.

LOUIE
That sorta rules out gettin' rich fast.

JAY
Some people do it.

LOUIE
Meaning who?

JAY
(shrugs) I just thought you could teach me some things.

LOUIE

I got nothin' to teach you and nothin' I want to teach you...*(angrily)* You think that's what I do? Rob banks? Rob liquor stores? Little old ladies in the park?

JAY

No. I don't think so.

LOUIE

(smiles) You got balls, kid. Did you know you got balls?

JAY

I'm aware of them, yes.

LOUIE

Take you with me for what? *(he heads for the bathroom)* For company? Your company is startin' to pester me already. What do I need you for? What can you do for me?

He goes into the bathroom and closes the door.

Jay thinks, looks at the black bag, points to it and calls out.

JAY

I could carry your little black bag.

Arty looks at him as if he made a mistake.

The door of the bathroom slowly opens and Louie comes out, looking more ominous than we've seen him thus far.

LOUIE

...You interested in my little black bag?

JAY

No. I just thought—

LOUIE

No, no, no, but you want to carry it. Why? Does it look heavy to you? You think I got a broken arm, I can't carry a little bag like that?

JAY

No.

LOUIE

No, maybe you got some other interest in it... Have you been foolin' around with that bag?

JAY

No, I swear.

LOUIE

No, but you're curious, right? How much it weighs or something? Why don't you pick it up, Jay? Go ahead, pick it up.

JAY

I don't want to pick it up.

LOUIE

Pick it up, Jay. It ain't gonna bite you. You're not gonna be happy till you pick it up... So pick it up!

JAY
I really don't want to.

ARTY
Jay, just pick it up.

JAY
You stay out of this.

LOUIE
No, no, no... Arty! Come here.

ARTY
Me?

LOUIE
That's right. You're Arty.

Arty gets up, slowly crosses to Louie.

LOUIE
I want you to come over to the table and pick up the bag.

ARTY
(looks over) Jay is closer.

LOUIE
Jay? Jay is not interested. I want you to do it.

Arty crosses to the table, looks at the bag.

LOUIE
Now, pick it up.

ARTY
I don't know why, but I think I'm going to cry.

When Jay asks to go along with his uncle to carry his bag, Louie (Richard Dreyfuss) begins to bully his nephews, who have no idea of the danger he's in. Jay will stand up to him and later help him get away— a turning point in courage for the fifteen-year-old.

LOUIE
Just pick it up, Arty.

Arty picks it up, turns.

LOUIE
Now, is it heavy?

ARTY
No.

LOUIE
Is it light?

ARTY
No.

LOUIE
So what is it?

ARTY
It's medium.

LOUIE
It's medium... Okay. Now what do you think is in that bag? Money?... Fives and tens and twenties and hundreds all wrapped together with rubber bands?... What?... I said what!!!

ARTY
I don't know.

LOUIE
You don't know... Well, then maybe you have to open up the bag and see...

ARTY
Please, Uncle Louie—

LOUIE
(steps closer) I'm only gonna ask you one more time, Arty. Because I'm runnin' outa patience... Open-the-bag!!

Arty looks at him helplessly, terrified.

JAY
Don't do it, Arty! Leave him alone, Uncle Louie... You want the bag open, do it yourself.

He puts it down carefully at Louie's feet.

JAY
Maybe you don't rob banks or grocery stores or little old ladies. You're worse than that. You pick on a couple of kids. Your own nephews. You make fun of my father because he cries and he's afraid of Grandma. Well, everyone in Yonkers is afraid of Grandma. And I'll tell you something else about my father. At least he's doing something in this war. He's sick and he's tired but he's out there selling iron to make ships and tanks and cannons. And I'm proud of him. What are you doing? Hiding in your mother's apartment, scaring little kids and acting like Humphrey Bogart. Well, you're no Humphrey Bogart... Yeah, and I'll tell you something else... No! That's all.

He sits. Louie stares at him, then takes two steps towards him. Jay leans away, frightened.

LOUIE
Jesus, that was good! That was terrific. I had tears in my eyes, I swear to God. You got bigger balls than I thought, Jay. You got a couple a steel basketballs there... Your father's a lucky guy, let me tell you. You know what you got, Jay? You got moxie.

JAY
What's moxie?

LOUIE
What's moxie? Tell him, Arty.

Arty does the same thing with his hands that Louie did before, that defiant, beckoning gesture.

ARTY
That's moxie.

Ext. Candy Store - Dusk
It is starting to get dark. The white sedan is parked on the street. Suddenly Harry and his brother get out. Harry motions for his brother to go one way, Harry goes in another direction.

Int. Bathroom - Dusk
Louie, dressed except for his jacket, is putting on after-shave lotion. The little black bag sits prominently on the sink. Grandma comes in, looks at the bag, then puts a bill on the sink next to the bag.

GRANDMA
You're getting careless, Louie. You dropped your money on my dressing table

She walks away.

Int. Living Room - Dusk
Louie follows her into the living room with the bill.

LOUIE
Louie's never careless, Ma. It's for you. I had a good week.

GRANDMA
A good week for you is a bad week for someone else. I don't want your profits, Louie.

LOUIE
It's just a hundred bucks. Get yourself a birthday present.

GRANDMA
Don't pay me for being born. I've been paid enough.

LOUIE
Then take it for putting me up. You know I hate hotels.

GRANDMA
(angrily) I don't take it from you! Not what you haff to give me... You were always the strongest one. The survivor. Live... at any cost, I taught you. But not when someone else has to pay the price. Keep your filthy money.

She throws it on the floor. Louie picks it up and smiles.

LOUIE

You're terrific, Ma. One hundred percent steel. Finest grade made. Eddie's out there lookin' for iron and the chump doesn't know he's got a whole battle-ship right here... Nah. You can't get me down, Ma. I'm too tough. You taught me good. And whatever I've accomplished in this life, just remember... you're my partner!

He throws her a ferocious kiss. She returns a venomous look.

Int. Kitchen - Night
We are on the sink. The leftovers are being scraped off the dishes. The dinner is over. As we pull back, we see Bella, Jay and Arty helping in the kitchen.

BELLA

I'll do that, Jay. Bring Aunt Gert her coffee. *(Jay goes)* Arty, put the nuts out on the table. *(she stops him)* How do you think everything is going so far?

ARTY

The potatoes were a little hard.

BELLA

Yeah, well, potatoes is not what I'm worried about.

Int. The Living Room - Night
Jay comes out and gives Aunt Gert her coffee. She is in her late thirties, a sweet but nervous woman, especially around Grandma. Arty puts the nuts on the table, taking one for himself. Bella comes out of kitchen. Louie looks at his watch, then gazes nervously out the side of the window. His black bag is ever present.

BELLA

Gert, would you like another piece of strudel with that?

GERT

(smiles) No.

BELLA

How about you, Louie? Another piece?

LOUIE

(edgy) No, I had enough, Bella. Thanks.

BELLA

You always have two pieces.

He is extremely nervous and irritable. He wants to get out. His hat and the black bag are on the table near the sofa.

LOUIE

No. One piece of strudel is enough tonight, Bella. Thank you.

He looks at his watch.

BELLA

Momma?

Bella starts to bring chairs from dining room into living room. Grandma is sitting in her usual club chair, doing some crocheting. Gert sits on the far end of the sofa, sipping her coffee.

More strudel is the last thing Louie wants as his showdown with Harry coincides with Bella's big announcement to their family after dinner. Richard Dreyfuss is Louie, Mercedes Ruehl is Bella.

BELLA
(bringing in chair) Don't help me with the chairs, anybody. I know exactly how I want this to be.

She puts one between the sofa and Grandma.

LOUIE
(gets hat and his bag) Momma, I'm gonna run along now. I'll call you next week. *(he crosses to Gert)*

He kisses her, puts on his hat and heads towards door.

LOUIE
Jay, don't worry about it. Arty! Keep your dukes up. Gert, great seeing you, sweetheart.

He's at the door.

BELLA
Louie, Louie, no. NOO!! You can't go yet. You promised.

LOUIE
I promised to stay for dinner. How many dinners do you want me to stay for?

BELLA
But the family hasn't had a talk yet.

LOUIE
We did. We talked all through dinner. I didn't get a chance to swallow nothin'.

BELLA

I know, but there's still something that hasn't been talked about. It wasn't something we could talk about at dinner. *(stands behind chair)* You sit here. This is your place.

LOUIE

(exasperated) I told you I had to go right after the coffee. I had my coffee. I had my strudel. I had my dinner. Bella, I gotta go.

BELLA

(nervously, to Grandma) Louie, you can't go. You have to be here. The whole family has to be here. Momma tell him!

GRANDMA

(without looking up) You're getting excited, Bella.

Bella catches herself quickly.

BELLA

(takes a breath) Alright, I won't get excited. I'm fine. Could you just ask him.

GERT

He'll stay, Bella.

BELLA

Okay. Jay! Arty! Sit on the sofa. Momma, you sit there. *(pointing to the chair she's already in, then crosses to chair on the other end of sofa)* I'll sit here and Louie, just sit on the chair.

Louie takes off his hat, angrily.

LOUIE

I've been sittin' all night, Bella. I think I'll stand, okay?

He stands behind his chair.

BELLA

Louie, it would be so much better if you were sitting. I pictured everybody sitting.

LOUIE

I don't wanna sit!! Change the picture. Picture everybody else sitting and me standing.

He crosses over to the other side of the room.

GERT

(gets up) Louie, can't you just sit for a few minutes till Bella tells us what— *(she sucks in her breath, squeezing the words out painfully)*—it is she wants to talk to us about.

Jay and Arty look at each other.

LOUIE

Okay. Okay. *(he sits on the window seat)* Here? Alright? Is this how you pictured it, Bella?

BELLA

(petulant) No. I pictured you sitting on the chair I picked out.

Aunt Gert (Susan Merson) knows trouble is brewing in the after-dinner scene. "You've been hearing about Gert and her speech impediment from the beginning," says director Martha Coolidge, "but how to introduce her in a movie way? In the play she's been sitting in the living room from the opening of the curtains. But here, you first see the back of her head, next a shot of her but she doesn't talk, and then she talks but normally, and you might've forgotten about it. But then—she breathes in."

Louie, fuming, crosses behind "his" chair but doesn't sit.

LOUIE
Bella, it's very important that I leave very soon. Very important. I don't want to get you upset, sweetheart, but I don't want to spend my time getting the seating arrangements right. I'm gonna stand up, I'm gonna listen and then I'm gonna go.

BELLA
(standing, sulks) I pictured everybody sitting.

LOUIE
Jesus!

GERT
Stop arguing with her and sit down for God's sakes before—*(she sucks in again)*—she gets into one of her moods again.

GRANDMA
Louie, quiet. Gertrude, stop it.

LOUIE
Louie, quiet! Louie, stay! Louie, eat! You don't scare me anymore, Ma. Maybe everyone else here, but not me, understand?

GRANDMA
(without looking up) Louie, sit!

Louie quickly sits. He is annoyed he gave in so easily.

BELLA
(cups her hands, looks around, finally contented) Okay...who wants to start?

Louie looks around like he was just committed.

In the big after-dinner scene dominated by Louie and Bella (Richard Dreyfuss and Mercedes Ruehl), **only Irene Worth as Grandma stays still.**

LOUIE

Who wants to start? Start what?... Momma, I don't got the time for this. Maybe when I was twelve years old, but not tonight. This is one of her games, Momma. You know, just one of her crazy games.

GERT

(turns to Bella) Is this a game, Bella? Are you just playing—*(sucks in words)*—a game with us, darling?

BELLA

No, no, no. This is not a game. It's very important. I just don't know how to start to say it. So somebody just has to help me out and start it first.

LOUIE

(to Bella) You've got something important to tell us and you want us to start? *(he gets up, grabs hat and bag again)* Gert No, no, no. You understand her better than me. When you figure out what it is, you let me know.

He starts for the door.

JAY

(to Bella, loud enough to stop Louie) Aunt Bella, have you —

Louie and the others look at Jay.

JAY

—have you been going to the movies lately, Aunt Bella?

BELLA

(like a gift from God, points to Jay) Yes! Thank you, Jay...I have been going to the movies a lot lately.

She looks at Louie. He stands there, waiting to hear the rest.

BELLA

...Three times last week.

JAY

Really? Did you see anything good?

BELLA

Yes. I saw a picture with William Holden and Jean Arthur. I really liked it. That's why I saw it three times.

LOUIE

This is what I stayed to dinner for? This is what I had to sit in the right seat to listen to? Jean Arthur and William Holden? Are they in the picture you pictured here?

GERT

Is that what this is about, Bella? Is this all about what movies—*(she sucks in)*—you went to see last week?

BELLA

No, no, no, but I'm getting to it. Jay, Jay, ask me more questions. Jay, c'mon.

JAY

Did you go alone?

BELLA

I did. I always go alone. But it's very interesting you would ask me that. Because I met a friend there... You can ask me questions too, Gert.

GERT

I don't know what kind of questions—*(she sucks in)*—to ask you.

ARTY

Ask her who the friend was.

GERT

(to Bella) Who was your friend?

BELLA

(to Gert) Well, his name is Johnny. I always see him there because he's the head usher. He's really nice.

JAY

So you just saw him in the theater?

BELLA

No, once or twice we went out for coffee and once we went for a walk in the park.

LOUIE

...You went to the park with this guy?

BELLA

Yeah, but just to talk... You have to sit down if you want to ask me questions, Louie.

Louie, annoyed and embarrassed, sits in his chair.

BELLA

Okay, whose turn is it now?

GRANDMA

Dis vas when you came home eleven o'clock?

BELLA

Yes. It was. Yeah. Thank you for listening, Ma.

GERT

What were you doing until eleven—*(sucks in)*—o'clock?

BELLA

Well, we walked and we talked. And we got to know each other. He doesn't want to be an usher forever. One day he wants to open up his own restaurant.

LOUIE

(mockingly) His own restaurant? And he's an usher? What is he, fifteen, sixteen?

BELLA

No, no, no. He's forty. And he wants to open up the restaurant with me.

There is stunned silence at that one.

110

LOUIE
Why with you?

BELLA
(getting nervous) Because I would...I would do all of the cooking...and I'd write out the menus...and I'd keep the books.

GERT
And what would he do?

BELLA
He would be the manager.

She sees this isn't going too well.

LOUIE
Wait, wait, wait. If he's the manager, then why doesn't he write out the menus and keep the books.

BELLA
(lowers her head and voice) 'Cause he has a reading handicap.

LOUIE
What?

BELLA
(a little louder) He has a reading handicap.

LOUIE
Wait, wait, wait. Hold it. Hold it a minute. *(he gets up)* What did you say? He can't read?

BELLA
You're not supposed to get out of your chair, Louie. That's not how I pictured it.

LOUIE
Well, maybe I'm getting my own little picture here... Now this guy is what? Illiterate?

BELLA
No, he can read...a little.

LOUIE
What does that mean, a little? His name? Now you listen to me. This guy is either pulling your leg or else he's after something. Now, is he after something?

BELLA
(starts to get out of her chair) Alright, maybe this isn't the right time to talk about this.

Louie rushes her.

LOUIE
No, I think it's a perfect time to talk about it. What is this guy after, Bella? *(aside to her)* Has he touched you? Has he fooled around with you?

BELLA
No! Louie, he's not that kind of person.

In 1992 Mercedes Ruehl won the two awards that actors most covet: a Tony for Best Actress for her performance as Bella in the play *Lost in Yonkers* and the Oscar for Best Supporting Actress for her part as Jeff Bridges's steadfast girlfriend in *The Fisher King*. Earlier, for her role as Connie, the madly jealous Mafioso housewife, in *Married to the Mob*, she received the American Film Critics Award as Best Supporting Actress. Off Broadway she was given the Clarence Derwent Award for her acting in *Other People's Money*, and she garnered an Obie for her part in Christopher Durang's *The Marriage of Bette and Boo*, a New York Shakespeare Festival Production.

Ruehl made her film debut in 1979, starring in Walter Hill's *The Warriors*; she has since appeared in *Another You* with Richard Pryor and Gene Wilder, *Big*, *Radio Days*, *Crazy People*, and *The Secret of My Success*, among other films.

(Opposite) **Bella** (Mercedes Ruehl) as we first meet her on the streets of Yonkers

MERCEDES RUEHL AS BELLA

Loving, eccentric, high-spirited, feather-witted Bella is the heart of *Lost in Yonkers*. She and her nephew Jay change psychologically more than any of their family as the drama of their summer of '42 unfolds. Mentally childlike, she has been kept at home to care for her crippled mother, the witch-like Grandma Kurnitz. But she stands up to Grandma, to let Jay and his brother Artie live with them, and then, her independence growing, she falls in love.

Will Johnny help Bella grow up and escape the candy store of enforced childhood? Will she defy Grandma, make peace with her, manage by herself? The Academy Award-winning actress Mercedes Ruehl plays Bella—in the film as she did on Broadway.

"When I first read the play, on my way to shoot *The Fisher King*, I thought it was a very charming and original piece, but I had no idea how to do the part. And I put it away for the whole shooting. Then I got a call saying, in two days you're to meet with Neil Simon and read these scenes from the play.

"I panicked, I thought oh my God, what do I do with her? do you talk baby talk? is she retarded? is she just slow? how bright is she—what? And I thought, oh, give me the script, because whatever I did, whether I got it or not, I didn't want to make a fool of myself in front of Neil Simon.

"So I took the script out one night and I looked at it and looked at it and studied it and read it. And I was alone in a hotel room in Marina del Rey, and I hope I didn't keep my neighbors up, because finally I poured myself a little glass of wine. . . . Suddenly I was out of my seat and I was talking to the furniture, and I was relating to Mama here and Louie over there and the bed was Eddie. But I still couldn't get it, and finally I thought, well, I need a metaphor for her.

"When I worked in *Big* with Tom Hanks, he was playing a thirteen-year-old in an adult's body. And the charming thing, which anchored it in reality, was that a thirteen-year-old really can pass as an adult. Maybe because we're all so immature essentially—although a thirteen-year-old is morally subtle and capable of humor. So I thought, oh, I'll make Bella similar. She didn't have to be some cartoon of a little girl talking baby talk—she was a full-blown human being whose emotional and intellectual life just stopped at about thirteen.

"For the film I've upped her age to about fifteen, sixteen. Well, I'm older myself now.

"That's how I began to relate to Bella, and then I began to have fun with her. And when you begin to have fun with a character, that's the kiss of the angels. So I got all these wonderful ideas cooking, and it was three o'clock in the morning, and I thought, I just hope I can remember them for Neil tomorrow.

"The next morning I got up and slammed on over to his office and he said, do you want to talk about the character, and I said no, I don't want to talk, I just want to do it for you, okay, and then you can just tell me it's wrong and I'll leave and we'll never meet again and I'll go teach acting at Oshkosh U. So he said okay, just do it. So I went and did it and I opened my mouth and this funny little person came out who had been born the night before.

"And he said, that's it."

(Opposite) **Bella listens intently to her nephews asking to come live with Grandma. Bella will insist they stay, over her mother's resistance—the first step in her growth to maturity.**

Fifteen-year-old Jay (Brad Stoll) **warns kid brother Arty** (Mike Damus) **not to touch Grandma's candy.**

The film is Stoll's first, and he must make several demanding—and amusing—speeches, as well as evolve from imitating Eddie, his timid father, to more genuinely adult independence and courage. A native of Old Bethpage, New York, on Long Island, Stoll has studied voice and acting, performed at Carnegie Hall, and appeared as a backup singer to country star Lee Greenwood at the 1992 Orange Bowl game.

Eddie (Jack Laufer) **tells his sons he has to become a traveling salesman to pay his late wife's hospital bill and must leave them with Grandma. That is, if she'll have them. Jay and Arty plead with him not to go, and later plead with Grandma to let them stay. Their different styles of poor persuasion create much of the comedy of this scene of fake filial devotion.**

(Opposite) **Irene Worth as Grandma**

"Sometime in the fifties I was given the Ibsen play John Gabriel Borkman, *and I had to play his wife, in a rigid and repressed family in Denmark, and I had to crochet. I didn't know how to do it. And I knew I'd never be able to get lessons quickly enough, so I went to a woman friend for help. She said, "Get a doily that's already made and then add little stitches around the edge. Everybody will think you made the whole thing." She showed me the basic stitch, and now I do it all the time. Mercedes and I were on Broadway for eight months doing this play, and my crocheting got larger and larger, and I had to rip it out three or four times and start over. It was rather fun."*
                                             —Irene Worth

"Grandma comes from the old European tradition of 'You will obey, you will work hard,"says Irene Worth. (Below) **She encourages Jay with her infamous cane.**

(Opposite) **Bella takes the boys to visit her siblings' resting place.**

"Bella is the youngest of Grandma's four surviving children, and she has what today would probably be called a disadvantage or mild handicap, but in 1942 she was considered retarded. Consequently she's been extremely protected and never allowed to grow up, though she has all the equipment. She's the heroine of this story, and like the innocent fool in a fairy tale, the character on the first Tarot card who journeys out on all the adventures in the deck, she learns the moral of the story." —Mercedes Ruehl

In their foldout bed—no refuge from Grandma—the adolescent brothers face grownup situations: they scheme to find Grandma's hidden money in order to lend it to their debt-ridden father, and they listen to Bella's excitement about her new boyfriend.

"Bella says Johnny is the only one she feels safe with. He's a soul mate, he's someone who's not trying to use her, who needs her. Meeting him gives her the path out of her relationship with her mother and into the world. Falling in love triggers the journey toward maturity. It often happens in people's lives—you break old ties and move into a new order. How you negotiate the transition is what this fairy tale is about."   —Mercedes Ruehl

(Below) **With Jay and Arty** (Brad Stoll and Mike Damus), **Uncle Louie** (Richard Dreyfuss) **sneaks out of Grandma's candy store, under the nose of mobster Hollywood Harry, who's waiting for him on the other side of this fence. The trio will go for a midnight swim, taunting Harry— who doesn't want to kill anybody, according to author Neil Simon, but does want the bag of payoffs that Louie plans to steal from him.**

(Opposite) **Louie** (Richard Dreyfuss) **feels the pressure from the waiting mobsters and is going to take it out on his adolescent nephews, who innocently want to team up with him and run away from Grandma's. The scene is a turning point in their relations: Jay will stand up to his uncle—and Louis will give him the ultimate kudo, "You got moxie, kid!"**

(Opposite above) *In the big after-dinner scene, Bella battles her protective family, and especially her brother Louie (Richard Dreyfuss), for her rights to a normal life.* "A camera picks up a whole realm of subtlety that is lost on the person in the back row of the mezzanine," *says Mercedes Ruehl.* "And so people say, keep it small and delicate —a glint in the eye communicates volumes, and it does. But I've found that the big, the theatrical, the grand stuff they say doesn't work on film does work—it's just got to be backed up, be fully true. Fully meant, totally honest."

(Opposite) **In the tea-making scene, Bella** (Mercedes Ruehl) **confronts her mother** (Irene Worth).

"We have a symbolic relationship, a mutual dependence that is keeping both of us from growing—from gaining wisdom and experience. I help Grandma run the store, I keep away the ultimate horror of total solitude, I keep her connected to others—the only character who does. Because she has alienated everyone else in the family. With the anger and the grief, which she keeps inside, which manifests itself as almost unbearable sternness." —Mercedes Ruehl

"It's not a good day today," says Johnny (David Strathairn), **and Bella understands that her infatuation with the handicapped movie usher is a movie fantasy, one she won't ever**

Against a background of pastel fences, **Aunt Gert** (Susan Merson) tells the boys that Bella, gone for four days, is staying with her. Her gasping speech problem, she admits, comes up mostly around Grandma.

The boys give Grandma a gift as they rush to meet their father and go home at last. Later, in her final shot in the film, she opens it, and we see her reaction to photographs of "Jakob and Artur." After all they've been through, how does she feel about her grandsons? The film lets us wonder.

Mercedes Ruehl recalls her final scene with Irene Worth (opposite): "Sometimes we'd say to each other, 'It's not a huge theater out there, why don't you try this for this moment?' Here I come in and sit down, there's a silence, everyone has left us, and we're once again alone in the house. Irene said, 'When you walk in, why don't you try sitting on the couch like this is the first time you've ever been in the room?' And I tried it and she was right—it's a whole new order for us, our relationship is different now."

(Overleaf) **Bella leaves home.**

"Bella understands her mother to some degree and Bella also needs her mother. Until the very end of this story, when Bella gets her own wings and flies, she feels like a lot of children that she can't exist without her parent, that she's totally dependent. But as all children do, as they mature from adolescence into young adulthood, she realizes that she doesn't need this person to live. She has what she needs to live by herself."

—Mercedes Ruehl

THE BOYS: BRAD STOLL AND MIKE DAMUS

"Brad Stoll and Mike Damus play Jay and Arty, and they were very new to acting," recalls director Martha Coolidge. "Though Mike had understudied Arty on Broadway, he had only gone on once. In the film, they worked with experienced actors and saw great acting every day. And every day I watched them learn something more about acting, about the affect of it, the interior work of it. They learned that it's not about pretending, or practicing to say a line, but how you feel about something. And they watched actors who are not only masters of that but can repeat the way they do things, over and over, and keep it alive.

"The boys brought their freshness and honesty to the film, because the one thing a young kid can't help being is real. They are full of new energy. And at the same time they have become experienced, and they say things like, 'I didn't like that take, no, that was a good one,' and 'Are you in my key light?'

"They were very hard to cast, because their roles are enormous and full of humor. They're in almost every scene. And I wanted them to be as authentic to New York as possible, but I couldn't ask them to learn New York accents on top of learning their characters, so we scoured the New York area. And we were very lucky.

"To work with adult actors, you want a child who can somehow feel it for real. And if you're playing a big scene and you look into their eyes, you want them to give it back to you. This give-and-take builds the scene. What I loved about Mike and Brad was that they got into the idea of living through the scene and playing off the other actors. They genuinely experienced it and let go a little, and they took the roller-coaster ride which acting is when you're really doing it. They are both wonderfully gifted.

"At age fifteen, Jay is halfway between being a boy and becoming a man. He needs to come out of this experience with Grandma knowing how to be courageous, how to stand up for what is right," says Coolidge. Brad Stoll, who plays Jay, remarks that "Jay is a very nervous character, always worried about doing the right thing. A little like his father that way, but less whining. Basically he takes care of Arty, and watches everything he does because Arty is mischievous. Jay is the older brother."

According to Mike Damus, who plays the thirteen-year-old younger brother, "Arty is almost the complete opposite of Jay. He's very laid back, he doesn't have many worries, because Jay takes care of him. He has a lot of fun. He has a dry sense of humor, and some days he spends trying to think how to escape from there, from the house we're forced to live in with our grandmother. The candy is like a force field—we can think about it but can't touch it. Or else, Grandma, Whacko! right over the head."

"Grandma treats Jay really bad," says Brad, "and always picks on him, because I look like my mother, who she didn't like at all. While she treats Arty so good. Until Uncle Louie comes along, it's just me and Arty. Then with Uncle Louie I have someone to talk to. He's so tough, and he can take on Grandma, and I really look up to him and want to become like him. But then he turns on me and yells at my brother and gets me really annoyed. But in all, I really respect him. He's just like my great uncle. We see Aunt Bella as our sister. Because she's really childlish, and we look at her like one of us."

"I hope kids can relate to us," Mike says. "It's a very funny script, it's just written by a genius. There are a lot of funny lines, and Arty especially gets a lot of one-liners. I think Jay sets up the joke and then Arty just piles it through. People will see that this aunt and uncle and grandma are such a crazy family, that you know you've got to like the kids.

"By living with them all this time, I think you learn that you can't judge people by the outside. Grandma is mean, but she has her reasons and she's not going to change. It's just that way—people are people, and you've got to learn to live with different kinds. A gangster uncle, a crazy aunt, and a vicious grandma. I think we adapted pretty well."

(Above) **Mike Damus and Brad Stoll** get executive producer Joe Caracciolo to bet on a card trick.

(Opposite) **Brad Stoll as Jay and Mike Damus as Arty** after school in **Yonkers**

129

LOUIE

What kind of person is he? He's forty years old, he takes you to the park at night. He wants to open up a restaurant with you and he can't read or write... And how are you going to open up a restaurant? Who's going to put up the money?

BELLA

It would only cost five thousand dollars.

LOUIE

(angrily) Five thousand dollars? Why not five million? And who's gonna put up the five grand? Him?

BELLA

No. I don't think so. He doesn't have any money.

LOUIE

Oh, too bad. Well, then who does that leave?

BELLA

Don't yell at me, Louie!

LOUIE

I'm not yelling at you, Bella. I'm asking you a question. Who does that leave to put up the five thousand dollars?

GERT

(stands) This is too terrible. Momma, please tell them—*(sucks in)*—to stop this awful thing.

LOUIE

Who does that leave, Bella?

BELLA

I'll get some money somewhere.

LOUIE

Where is somewhere, Bella? There is no somewhere. You want Momma to sell the store? Is that what this guy asked you to do?

BELLA

No. He didn't ask me anything.

LOUIE

Well, either this guy is very, very smart or he's very dangerous. And he don't sound smart to me. So that only leaves dangerous.

BELLA

He's not dangerous.

LOUIE

How do you know?

BELLA

(angrily) They don't take you at the Home if you're dangerous.

GRANDMA

Oh, my Gott!!

Richard Dreyfuss as Louie and Mercedes Ruehl as Bella let fly in the after-dinner scene.

130

LOUIE

The HOME??

GERT

I don't understand this. Can somebody please—*(sucks in)*—explain this all to me.

LOUIE

Bella, honey. This man sounds very troubled. Is he staying at the Home now?

BELLA

No. He lives with his parents. He didn't like the Home. They weren't all that nice to him there. *(pointedly to Momma)* Momma, that's not a nice place over there.

LOUIE

Bella, sweetheart. I don't want you going to the movies anymore. I do not want you to see this particular fella anymore. He may be very nice but he sounds like he's got a lot of whacky ideas, you know what I'm saying, sweetheart?

BELLA

(to boys on sofa) Jay! Arty! You said you would back me up here. C'mon, you promised.

LOUIE

Back you up with what? With the restaurant? With the money? Is that what this guy's after?

BELLA

No, Louie, he wants more than that.

LOUIE

What could possibly be more than that, Bella?

BELLA

Me!! He wants me. He wants to marry me. I want to marry him! I want to have his children. I want my own babies.

LOUIE

Jesus Christ!

GRANDMA

Dot's enough. I don't want to hear this anymore.

BELLA

Why, you think that I can't have healthy babies, Momma? I can. I'm as strong as an ox. I've worked in that store and taken care of you by myself since I was twelve years old, that's how strong I am...like steel, Momma. Isn't that what you say we're supposed to be? Only my babies won't die because I will love them and I will take care of them... My babies will be happy because I will teach them to grow and be happy. And not to grow up and run away and never visit when they're older and not to be so frightened that they couldn't even breathe...and never, ever to make them spend their lives rubbing my back and my legs because you never had anybody around who loved you enough to want to touch you because you made it so clear you just didn't want to be touched...with love... Do you know what it's like to touch steel, Momma? It's hard and it's cold and I don't want that for my babies. I want to be soft and warm. Momma, let me have babies, because I gotta love somebody. I gotta love somebody who'll love me back before I die... And I promise you, you would never worry about being alone 'cause you'd have us... Louie, tell her how wonderful that could be... Gert, wouldn't that make her happy? Wouldn't it? *(she crosses to Momma, kneels on stool.)*

It is deadly silent. No one has moved. Finally, Grandma gets up, helped by her cane, turns and walks without a word to her door, opens it, goes in and closes it.

BELLA
Momma, please say yes...Momma, momma, I need you to say yes... Please. Somebody please hold me... Please hold me.

Gert holds Bella in her arms, sobbing, and rocks her gently.

Ext. Street - Candy Store - Night
It is late that night. We see Hollywood Harry's car parked across the street from the store. It is dimly lit We hear Jay's voice-over.

JAY (V.O.)
"Dear Pop, Later that night, something happened that I know you wouldn't approve of. I hope you will forgive me—"

The light goes out on the neon bar sign.

HARRY
The bar's closed

A man stumbles out of the bar and walks across the street.

BROTHER
Look at this guy.

We see a figure in the dark, wearing a hat, topcoat and carrying the black satchel. He comes out of the back door of the house and starts to move away swiftly. Harry and his brother see the figure and run down the street after him.

BROTHER
Hey.

In a flash, they grab the figure and the bag, throwing him against the wall.

HARRY
Where the hell do you think you're going?

The light hits the figure's face. It is Jay, petrified. Harry opens the satchel and looks inside. It's got shirts and socks in it. He takes them out and throws them on the street.

BROTHER
Harry, it's empty.

HARRY
Where is he? Where's my money?

JAY
What money?

HARRY
(slaps Jay in the face) My goddamned money.

JAY

I don't know what you're talking about. I found the bag in the house. I was running away from home.

Harry pulls his gun out and sticks it on Jay's face.

HARRY

You tell me where he is or this is where you stop running.

JAY

(cries) I don't know. I swear.

Harry, fuming with anger, kicks the satchel hard, throws Jay against the wall. He falls to the ground, sobbing.

HARRY

I'm gonna find him, kid. And I'm gonna find the money. And if not, you better pray you don't never see me again.

Hollywood Harry's car across the street.

We see Louie in the car. He starts the motor, honks the horn and waves the satchel out the window, with a big smile.

LOUIE

(calls out) Harry. I'll send your car back in an envelope!... Thanks, Jay Jay! You got moxie, kid.

He laughs and drives off.

Hollywood Harry shoots his gun at Louie.

He stands there fuming.

HARRY

He had two bags. The son of a bitch had two bags.

Jay, lying on the ground as Harry and his brother storm off.

JAY (V.O.)

"I know it was wrong for me to help Uncle Louie get away, Pop, because he was a crook. But after what I saw Grandma do to Aunt Bella tonight, I thought someone in this family ought to help somebody else."

Ext. School - Day
Arty and Jay carrying school books are on their way home, passing other kids from school. No one pays attention to them.

JAY

(to Arty, as they walk) Where do you think Aunt Bella could be? Gone four days, somewhere in the city. I'm worried.

ARTY

Maybe Uncle Louie took her with him?

JAY

If he didn't take me, you think he's going to take Aunt Bella and her forty-year old usher from the Home?

Ext. House - Back Porch - Day
As they approach the back entrance, Aunt Gert is coming out.

Jay's movie fantasy of mobsters and stolen money comes to life as Hollywood Harry (Robert Guy Miranda) **nabs** Jay (Brad Stoll) **while Uncle Louie escapes.**

JAY

Hi, Aunt Gert. How's Grandma?

GERT

She looks tired. But she wouldn't even let me—*(sucks in breath)*—help her in the store.

JAY

Any idea where Aunt Bella is?

GERT

(looks around, whispers) She's at my house. She doesn't want anyone— to know.

ARTY

Is she ever coming back?

GERT

Who knows? She's meeting with—*(sucks in breath)*—that man today. *(she coughs)* I'm sorry. It's hard for me to talk.

JAY

Isn't there something the doctors can do for it?

GERT

I don't have it that much. It's mostly—*(sucks in breath)*—when I come here. I'll call you, tonight. Bye, honies.

She kisses both boys and leaves.

Ext. Riverbank - Day
Bella stands there, looking into the water, biting her thumbnail backwards, holding her purse tightly in her hands. Suddenly Johnny appears. Bella turns, smiles.

BELLA

Hi, Johnny. *(he nods slightly)* ...I guess you've been wondering why you haven't seen me in a few days?

JOHNNY

(nods) We have a new Bette Davis picture tonight.

BELLA

I've got more things on my mind than Bette Davis... I haven't been home in four days, I might never go back.

JOHNNY

Henry Fonda's in this one.

BELLA

Johnny, listen to me. 'Cause this is important... We can open up the restaurant any time you want. I've got the money. Five thousand dollars. I've got it right here in my purse.

He is fidgety, getting very nervous.

JOHNNY

Mr. Margolis said...he said he might be opening another theater soon... A—a bigger one.

BELLA

Yeah, but you don't want to be an usher forever. You told me that... You know what? I even found a place. It's right next to a bowling alley. People get hungry when they bowl.

Johnny keeps shaking his head from side to side, without stopping, relentlessly.

BELLA

...What, you don't want it? You afraid of running a restaurant?

He can hardly catch his breath. He keep stepping from side to side, looking away from her.

BELLA

...Because I told you, I'll do most of it.

She can see he's in a panic.

BELLA

Okay, okay, okay... Listen, usher's a good job... Maybe if the theater is bigger, you would make more money.

JOHNNY

I have to go.

BELLA

Why? Why?

JOHNNY

I have to go.

BELLA

Why? Because of me? Is that what your parents want you to do? Because I never really got a chance to talk to them.

JOHNNY

It's just not a good day, today.

BELLA

Not a good day? It's not a good day to open a restaurant? It's not a good day to get married? It's not a good day to have a baby? It's not a good day for any of that?

He starts to cry, hiding his face in his hands.

BELLA

Oh, God! Don't start... Don't cry. It's alright.

He continues to cry. She holds his face in her hands, comforting him.

BELLA

...You don't have to do anything you don't want to do. I promise... I would never do that to you.

She holds him.

Ext. Back Porch - Day
Grandma sits on the back porch, snapping beans. Suddenly she senses the presence of someone. She turns. Bella is standing there. She is wearing a jacket and a hat, carrying a suitcase and cake box.

The San Francisco-born actor holds his M.A. from Williams College, where he was a classmate of film-maker-novelist John Sayles. Sayles cast him in his first feature, the 1979 *Return of the Secaucus Seven*, and the 1984 *Brother from Another Planet*, in addition to *Matewan*, *Eight Men Out* and *Passion Fish*. He has also appeared in Mike Nichols's *Silkwood* (1983), and he starred in *Iceman* and *City of Hope*.

In theater, Strathairn has appeared in the Broadway production *Einstein and the Polar Bear*, the off-Broadway staging of Sam Shepard's *A Lie in the Mind*, and works at the Public Theater and National Theatre. His television credits include starring roles in *Day One* (as Robert Oppenheimer) and *Son of the Morning Star* (as Custer) and in Hallmark Hall of Fame and American Playhouse presentations.

DAVID STRATHAIRN, BELLA'S JOHNNY

It may take a special intelligence to play dumb. Certainly there are special challenges in the new role of Johnny, Bella's movie-usher beau, which Neil Simon added to the film.

"Johnny works in the local movie theater," comments David Strathairn, who won the part. "And he has probably reached his level of competency in the job market. He lives at home with his parents, in a way parallel to Bella, but with love and support—something it would be hard for him to leave. He isn't adept enough mentally to move out on his own into the community.

"Johnny is a 'friend' of Bella's—there are romantic possibilities, but because of who they are, this takes on an eccentric separate life. He offers a bit of hope for Bella, that she might be able to go out, have a relationship, a family of her own. But for reasons you see in the film, it's obvious why they can't or don't. They probably could have, but not in 1942.

"I wasn't sure how far to go with Johnny's mental condition. If he's truly retarded, then he would have been in the Home, but if he's too much aware, then why the problem with Bella? So the tone hovers—there's a deep sadness to the relationship but it's also very sweet. There's a meeting on some intangible wave length they both happen to be on.

"To research the role, I contacted Maureen Gallagher, who is part of the Association for Retarded Citizens in Poughkeepsie, New York. It's tied in with a rehabilitation center for the physically handicapped and somewhat more mentally disturbed. People like Johnny work at their kitchen—people who live with their family or in group homes. There they're taught jobs like serving food and working cash registers. On the surface, they look like anybody else on the street, and they're capable of holding jobs. But they can't handle too much at any given time. There's a lack of inhibition, and sometimes their emotions run at right angles to the situation they're in. I spent some time observing, thanks to Maureen.

"Johnny lives in the movies as much as Bella does, and so he goes along with the fantasy of having a family, but when this actually drops into reality, it becomes a major tremor. His silence in their previous scenes gives consent to her hopes and lets her go ahead. . . and that leads to act three.

"In broad strokes, the theme of the piece is the resiliency of the human spirit. These people could be much more dysfunctional and tragically damaged. Yet like grass in a concrete sidewalk, their life goes on. I'm not sure the ending is happy, but it's full of understanding of people. For Bella has chosen to focus on the hopeful, the bright, her nephews, youth—the loving side."

David Strathairn is a highly regarded stage actor who has been recognized for his screen roles as well, notably as the blind computer technician in *Sneakers* and the team owner in *A League of Their Own*. Television audiences know him as the bookseller in the series *The Days and Nights of Molly Dodd*.

IRENE WORTH AS GRANDMA KURNITZ

What child hasn't heard the words, "You'll sit there until you finish eating that!" and "I don't want that trash in my house!" and "Are you paying my electrical bills?" Grandma Kurnitz hisses these lines and more, freezing her nephews and daughter Bella with the timeless terror of being Bad Children. But as written by Neil Simon and played by the distinguished stage and screen actress Irene Worth, Grandma is not only a familiar disciplinarian but an archetypal kind of survivor, a Jewish immigrant who denies her own grief and guilt about the loss of family members and so denies all other emotions.

"I don't like her, no, I don't like her at all," says Worth, who received a Tony and a Drama Desk Award for her stage performance as Grandma Kurnitz. "I wouldn't stay in the same room with her for five minutes. She's bound into rigid behavior, there's fear in everything she does. But I do understand her.

"She's the head of the family because her father was killed in a political uprising; her husband died and so did her first two children; she is left with debts and alone, and she's incapacitated with her limp, and she has to bring up the rest of her children with the candy store.

"But Grandma is tough. She comes from the old European tradition: 'You will behave, you will not talk back, you will work hard.' Industry and all the great virtues she believed in to the letter. So she's very hard on her children and people think she's cruel. I think she's needlessly severe and yet, when I was doing the play, every night somebody would come up to me at the stage door and say, 'You're just like my grandmother' or 'You remind me of my mother.' And they would say these things not in a reproachful way, but simply as a confirmation that a great many people recognize this woman.

"Grandma is old," says the veteran actress. "She initially rejects her grandchildren because she's too tired. When you see the candy store, it's incredible, a fairy land, but you also see her going up and down the stairs all the time, with a cane, and it's a tremendous tear on her spinal column and general nerve.

"She doesn't want to take those grandchildren in, because she has to feed them, see that they stay well—it's bringing up children all over again. Most grandparents want their grandchildren around, but the relief to them is that they're not around all the time. That's why they are so adorable. So she rejects them.

"Do I think Grandma learns by the end to show a little bit of love? If I did think so, I wouldn't tell you, because I don't want to give an interpetation of this play. It has to be received and interpreted by every person who comes to see it."

Irene Worth is an Honorary Commander of the British Empire, by appointment of Queen Elizabeth II. The actress received the Antoinette Perry Award for Distinguished Achievement in the Theatre in 1965, and an Obie for a lifetime of Outstanding Achievement in the Theatre in 1989. In addition to the Tony for Best Supporting Actress for her performance in *Lost in Yonkers,* she won Tony awards for Best Actress in *Tiny Alice* in 1965 and again in *Sweet Bird of Youth* in 1975. She holds three Obie awards, including Best Actress in *The Cherry Orchard* (1977) and *Happy Days* (1979).

Educated at UCLA, Worth made her Broadway debut in 1943, and soon moved to England where she became a noted Shakespearean actress as a member of the Old Vic, Royal Shakespeare Company and Royal National Theatre repertories. In 1966 she won the London Evening Standard Award for her performance opposite Noel Coward in *Suite in Three Keys*, which he wrote for her and himself. For her role in *Heartbreak House* in 1967 she won the Variety Club of Great Britain Award and the Whitbread Anglo-American Award for Outstanding Actress.

Though her film appearances were infrequent, Worth won the British Film Academy Award for Best Woman's Performance in her 1957 screen debut, *Orders to Kill.* She has also starred in the British thriller *The Scapegoat* (1971), *Eyewitness* (1980) with William Hurt, Sidney Lumet's *Deathtrap* (1982) and *Fast Forward* (1985), directed by Sidney Poitier.

Irene Worth as Grandma broods on the back porch: Bella has been gone for four days.

BELLA
Hello, Momma.

Grandma doesn't acknowledge her and keeps working the beans.

BELLA
I bought you a coffee cake from Greenbaum's. It's still warm.

GRANDMA
You're home for goot or dis is a visit?

BELLA
I don't know. I thought I'd come back and talk to you about that.

GRANDMA
The way you talked to me da night you left? Vidout a word?

BELLA
No! Not without a word. I told you how I felt. You were the one that walked out on me, Momma.

GRANDMA
I heard what you had to say. I didn't haff to hear more.

BELLA
Momma, look at me, Momma. Momma, look at me. I'm not crying. And it's not because I'm afraid to cry. It's 'cause I have no tears left in me. I feel pretty empty inside. Like you feel all the time.

GRANDMA
How vould you know how I feel?

She gets up and heads up the stairs as Bella follows.

BELLA
You don't think I know anything, do you? You think I'm stupid, don't you, Momma?

GRANDMA
(going up) No. You're not stupid.

BELLA
Then what? Am I crazy? Do you think I'm crazy?

GRANDMA
(sharply) Don't use dot word to me.

BELLA
Why not? Are you afraid of it? Momma, if that's what I am, don't be afraid to say it. Because if I'm crazy, I should be in the Home. Then you'd be alone and you wouldn't like that. Is that why you don't use that word, Momma? Is it?

Grandma opens the back door and goes into the hall.

Int. Hall - Day
Grandma starts for the kitchen as Bella follows her.

BELLA
Is it?

GRANDMA
(stops, looks at her) You vant to know vot you are, Bella? You're a child. Dot's vot da doctors told me. Not crazy. Not stupid. You're a child... And dot's how I treat you. Because that's all you understand. You don't need doctors. You don't need to live in da Home. Dis is vere you live. Vere you can be vatched and taken care of. You will always be a child. Und in dis vorld vere dere is so much hate und sickness und death, den maybe you're better off. You stay a child, Bella, und be glad dot's what Gott made you.

She crosses into kitchen, leaving Bella behind.

Int. Kitchen - Day
Grandma lights the stove under a kettle of water. Bella comes into the kitchen.

BELLA
Then why did he make me look like a woman? And feel like a woman inside? And want all the things a woman should have? Is that what I am supposed to thank him for? ...Momma, I know that I get confused sometimes...and I know that I get frightened... But if I'm a child, why can't I be happy like a child? Why can't I be satisfied with dolls instead of babies?

GRANDMA
I'm not so smart I can answer such things.

BELLA
But I am smart. Maybe only as smart as a child, but some children are smarter than grownups. Some grownups I've seen are very stupid. And very mean.

GRANDMA
You don't have responsibilities, Bella. It's responsibilities vot makes meanness.

BELLA
I don't want to be your responsibility!!

GRANDMA
Den who vill be responsible for you? Yourself? Dot man you ran away vith?

In their last confrontation, Bella challenges her mother (Irene Worth).

She pours water into a cup and puts it in a teaball.

GRANDMA
Who vants money from you? Und Gott only knows vot else. Things you vould never know about. Stay the way you are, Bella, because you don't know vot such feelings vould do to you.

She crosses out of the kitchen with her teacup.

Int. Dining Room - Day
Bella follows her out. Grandma sits at table and stirs her tea.

BELLA
Yes, I do, Momma. I know what other things you're talking about. Because they've happened to me... They've happened because I wanted them to happen...

GRANDMA
(sips her tea) You're angry so you tell me lies. I don't vant to hear your childish lies.

BELLA
(grabs Momma's hands to stop her from drinking) When I was in school, I let boys touch me. And boys that I met in the park. Some nights when you were sleeping, I went down and I let them in... And not just boys... Men too.

GRANDMA
Stop dis. You dream dis stuff in your head.

BELLA
I needed somebody to hold me. To tell me that I was pretty. You never once told me that. Some of them even told me that they loved me. Alright... Alright, alright, I know what they really wanted... Except Johnny... And I thought for the first time in my whole life maybe I could be happy. So that's why I ran away. I even brought him the five thousand dollars for the restaurant.

GRANDMA
(disdainfully) Is dis something else you dreamed of? Vere vould you get five thousand dollars?

Bella opens the purse and takes out a roll of bills tied together with a rubber band and puts it on the table.

GRANDMA
Where did you get this? Huh?

BELLA
Does this look like a dream, to you?

Grandma picks up the money, looking at it, disbelieving.

GRANDMA
(she looks back towards her room) Did you steal from me? You know vere I keep my money. You are the only one.

She throws the tea from her cup at Bella.

GRANDMA
You thief! You steal from your own mother? You thief!!

Facing Grandma at the table, Mercedes Ruehl as Bella, her dreams shattered, has gained the determination and self-awareness of an adult.

Grandma (Irene Worth) **thinks Bella has stolen her savings.**

She picks up her cane at her side and raises it towards Bella. Bella grabs it.

BELLA

Do it! Now do it! Do it! Hit me. Crack my head open. Make me stupid and crazy. That's what you really think I am, isn't it? Isn't it?

GRANDMA

Get out of my house! You go live with your thief friend.

Bella rushes and puts on her coat, grabbing her bag.

GRANDMA

You vant da rest of my money, go...go take it. It von't last you long. You'll both haff to steal again to keep alive, believe me.

BELLA

I don't want your money. Here... Here, you take that. Louie gave it to me. Maybe he's a thief too, but he's my brother and he cared enough to want to help me... Thieves and sick little girls, that's what you got. Only God didn't make them that way... You did!!...You! We're alive, but that's all we are... Rose and Aaron are the lucky ones.

GRANDMA

Nooo! Don't say dot!... Gott, don't say dat to me.

BELLA

I'm sorry... I didn't mean to hurt you like that.

GRANDMA

Yes. You do. It's my punishment for being alive...for surviving my own children... For not dying before them that is my sin... Go on. Take Louie's money. You tink I don't know vot he is? He stole since he was five years old. The year Aaron died. And I closed off from him und from everybody... I lost Rose und then I lost Aaron, und I couldn't stand losing no more. Go open your restaurant. Live your own life. Haff your babies. If it's a mistake, let it be your mistake. If I've done wrong by you, den it's for me to take care of.

BELLA

There is no restaurant, Momma... He's afraid to be a businessman. He likes being an usher. He doesn't want babies. He doesn't want to get married... He just wants to live with his parents because he knows that they love him...and that's enough for him.

GRANDMA

Den maybe he's more lucky than you.

BELLA

(she gets up) Yeah, but I can't stop wanting things. It can't be the same between us anymore, Momma. It can't. *(she picks up her suitcase)* I'm gonna put my things away. I think we've both said enough for today... Don't you?

She looks at Grandma, then crosses into her bedroom and closes the door.

We cut back to Grandma. She sits in her chair. The camera moves in on her slowly. She is confused, hurt, destroyed... And as we move in closer, she takes out her handkerchief to muffle a cry or a scream...a scream so terrifying that it cannot be heard.

Ext. A Ferry - On a River - Day
Eddie stands next to the railing, looking out. He takes a postcard from his inside pocket and looks at it again. We hear Bella's voice-over.

BELLA (V.O.)

"Dear Eddie...I'm just writing to tell ya that Jay and Arty are fine. But something's happening to me that I can't figure out. Lately, I feel so happy and so sad at the same time. Did you ever feel that way? I'd tell you more, but I don't have anymore room. Love, Bella."

Ext. Rooftop - Day
Arty and Jay on the flat roof, leaning on the edge, looking out.

JAY (V.O.)

Then one night, Uncle Louie called Aunt Bella. He said he didn't know if he could ever come back to Yonkers again, but he was doing great in Guadalcanal. Grandma didn't say anything because she didn't come down to dinner that night... Eight months later, we got a card from Pop saying he was coming home to get us.

ARTY

(looking out) Jay, come here. There he is! That's him. It's Pop!

Ext. Street - Candy Store - Day
In the distance we see Pop's borrowed car coming down the road.

Ext. Rooftop - Day

ARTY

Come on, let's go.

They run off.

Int. Living Room - Day
Grandma, in her chair crocheting. The boys come running out, past Grandma, heading for the stairs.

ARTY

He's here, Grandma. Pop is here.

On a ferry somewhere in the South, Eddie (Jack Laufer) reads a postcard from Bella.

GRANDMA
You stop right now, you hear me?

ARTY
But Pop is—

GRANDMA
You vant to say good-bye to me, you say it now.

JAY
We're not leaving this minute.

GRANDMA
You came here quick, you say good-bye quick.

The boys look at each other.

JAY
Yes, Grandma... I...er...I just want to say thank you for taking us in. I know it wasn't easy for you.

GRANDMA
Dot's right. It vasn't.

JAY
(with some spunk) Well, it wasn't easy for us either.

GRANDMA
Ohh! You're not afraid to say the truth. Dot's goot. Maybe you learned something here.

Jay motions to Arty, then they both cross to her and each kiss her on the cheek.

GRANDMA
Maybe now I get some rest.

Arty goes in his pocket and gives her a gift. Arty and Jay start for the door.

GRANDMA
(without looking at them) Vot vere you two looking for dot night under the ice cream? My money maybe?

The boys look at each other guiltily.

ARTY
No. I swear.

GRANDMA
Don't swear!! You lie to me, you lie to everybody.

ARTY
Yes, Grandma.

They cross the door and open it.

GRANDMA
It was in da mattress you vere sleeping on.

They both realize what idiots they were, and leave. Grandma gets up, goes to the window and looks out.

As Arty and Jay (Mike Damus and Brad Stoll) **leave her, Grandma has the last word.**

147

Ext. Street - Grandma's Point of View - Day
We are looking down the street. We see the car pull up. Eddie rushes out and the boys run into his arms, all embracing, hugging, kissing each other. Eddie looks up.

Ext. Street - Candy Store - Eddie's Point of View - Day
We see Grandma at the window. When she is seen, she moves away from it.

Ext. The Street - Day
Bella is half-walking, half-running, down the street. She carries her purse and a large brown paper bag in her arms.

BELLA
Eddie, wait! Jay! Arty! Don't go yet.

She rushes to them.

EDDIE
Bella *(he embraces her)* It's so good to see you, sweetheart. You look wonderful.

BELLA
Yeah, I do? I lost ten pounds.

EDDIE
Well, it looks great.

BELLA
Really? 'Cause I put it back on a month ago.

Rescued: Eddie (Jack Laufer) **has paid off his debts and here is joyfully reunited with his sons.**

EDDIE
I'd better go up and see Momma. Thank you for everything, Bella.

He kisses her and goes into the house.

BELLA
(to boys) Alright. Close your eyes, both of you. Close them.

They both close their eyes. She takes out a leather basketball and a pigskin football from the bag, holding one in each hand.

She holds them up, looking at them, then gives Jay the football.

BELLA
The basketball is for Jay.

He takes it. She gives Arty the basketball.

BELLA
And the football is for Arty... Do you like them?

ARTY
Holee mackerel.

JAY
This is incredible.

BELLA
Well, I didn't know if I got the right size, so I just took a guess.

Arty and Jay (Mike Damus and Brad Stoll) **wave good-bye to Bella.**

JAY

Well, back up... Let's throw it around.

BELLA

Okay, okay, but don't throw too high.

The camera moves back as the boys start to toss the football to each other, including Bella in the game.

JAY (V.O.)

As hard as it was coming to live with Grandma, it was twice as hard leaving Aunt Bella. Because in the ten months since we came, she lost Johnny, she lost Uncle Louie and now she was losing me and Arty.

Ext./Int. Car - Candy Store - Day
The car pulls away. Eddie is driving, Arty and Jay leaning out the window and waving good-bye.

Bella

She stands on the street alone, waving good-bye, as the camera pulls away from her. We see the car drive off.

Int. Living Room - Day
Grandma is in her chair, doing her crocheting, as if nothing had changed in the house. Bella comes in from downstairs, looking a little forlorn. She sits on the couch. There is only silence.

BELLA

Well, I'll get dinner started...would you mind eating early, Momma? I'm going out with a friend.

Grandma doesn't look up.

BELLA

A girl...I got a new girlfriend. She likes me and I like her.

Grandma nods as if to say "more trouble"...

BELLA

...And she also has a brother that I like... He works in the library... He can read everything.

She starts for the kitchen again, stops and turns.

BELLA

...Do you think maybe during dinner, we could listen to some music on the radio, Ma? *(no answer)* ...It doesn't have to be tonight... Just think about it. Okay?

Bella crosses into the kitchen. Grandma looks after her. She then opens the gift from the boys. It is a homemade card with a picture of Jay and Arty with their writing "Love Jakob and Artur."

Int. Kitchen - Day
Bella starts to prepare dinner

Bella (Mercedes Ruehl) **has a new friend, she tells Grandma, with a brother.**

150

JAY (V.O.)
I wish I could say that while Aunt Bella started to make dinner, music came from the living room... But it didn't. But then Aunt Bella didn't really expect it. She was learning you could become strong in life without having to become like steel.

Int. Kitchen & Living Room - Early Morning
The room is empty.

Int. Candy Store - Early Morning
It is empty

Ext. House and Street - Early Morning
The street is still, quiet, empty.

JAY (V.O.)
...And then one day, early on a Sunday morning, the most unexpected thing happened.

We see Bella appear, coming out of the house in a coat, hat and carrying a suitcase.

JAY (V.O.)
...Aunt Bella left home... People who saw her from the window that day said she looked a little scared... Maybe she just wanted to go somewhere where she could hear the music.

We hear music come up as Bella walks down the street. Bella walks on as the music comes up.

Fade out.

End titles

(Opposite) **Bella leaves home.**

In the last shot of the film, shown in Maurice Zuberano's illustration, the streets of Yonkers are fresh and full of possibilities.

Shelley Komarov received Emmy awards for her designs for the 1986 television series *Peter the Great* and the 1990 series *Kennedy of Massachusetts*. Among her twenty-six films, perhaps her best-known designs clothed "Jacqueline Kennedy" in the 1992 television series, *A Woman Named Jackie*, a special that earned Komarov an Emmy nomination.

The Russian-born designer holds a Master's degree in science and economics from Leningrad Industrial Engineering College. By 1980, when she and her husband, Boris, emigrated to the United States, she was an established costume designer, with honors for her work for the Kirov Ballet and the Soviet Opera Company. In Russia, she won the prestigious Leningrad Award as well as the USSR's National Award for Design.

COSTUMING THE "YONKERS" CAST

It's the first take of Bella's first scene with Jay and Arty in the candy store, and she is concocting magnificent towering hot-fudge sundaes for her beloved nephews. In character as the gawky, energetic Bella, Mercedes Ruehl accidently wipes a chocolate-smeared hand on her pale pink dress—CUT! This stain is not in the script, and if the scene has to be reshot, a stain that appears in one frame and not in the next will disrupt the film's continuity. Shelley Komarov's department speeds to the rescue.

Komarov, costume designer for *Lost in Yonkers*, is ready. Guarding against anything that would halt shooting and mean expensive delays, Komarov's seamstresses had prepared "doubles and triples" in costumes for all the principal actors: the nine unique vintage buttons on Bella's stained dress are removed and resewn onto its replica, and the new garment is rushed back to the set.

The Emmy-winning costume designer had completed her creative work long before location shooting began. She consulted with David Chapman, production designer, about the dominant color harmonies of the sets, and with cinematographer Johnny Jensen about the actors' places and lighting; she researched period art and media— especially the Sears, Roebuck catalogue—for styles of the early 1940s, and she took the taste of 1993 into account. "When you design for period films, you always have to remember that the clothes have to appeal to contemporary people," she says. "The challenge is to achieve both period accuracy and current charm."

Komarov also considered how their dress expresses the characters in *Lost in Yonkers* and their changes through the story. Bella, she says, "must look attractive, but this big woman is a child. So all of her waistlines are a little high, as if she has outgrown her clothes. She is good with her hands, so she is supposed to have made that pink dress herself—she embroidered pink elephants on it. The pastel colors convey how young and vulnerable she is. Only later when she is more mature and womanly, in the last scenes, does she wear bright or dark colors—a red and blue print in the after-dinner scene, black-and-white in her last scene with Grandma.

"Grandma is an old German who doesn't spend money on clothes. She uses them over and over again, and makes aprons out of the old dresses. Her black-and-white print garments are timeless. She'll wear them to the end of her life.

"The gangsters, on the other hand, are the most flamboyant dressers—we hand-painted Hollywood Harry's Betty Grable and other ties. Uncle Louie is trying to be upscale like that and to impress the boys, but he hasn't quite made it. In the after-dinner scene, though, he wears a dapper going-away suit, top coat and hat."

Komarov and her team also outfitted a total of 1500 extras, divided between the Cincinnati area locations and the Los Angeles set. "The candy store neighborhood had one look," she says, "the movie theater crowd another."

STILL PHOTOGRAPHER ZADE ROSENTHAL

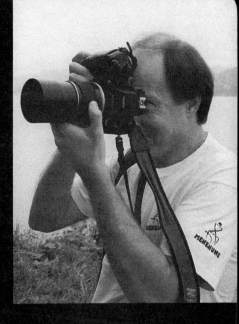

Without Zade Rosenthal's photographs, this book would be very different. Jewel-like saturated colors, sensitive framing of each image and engaging portrayals of people are the signature of all his movie images, which closely resemble the frames of the films but also have independent appeal. While photographs by Marc Wavra and Jane O'Neal are also reproduced here, the lion's share are by Rosenthal, who was the primary still photographer for *Lost in Yonkers*. He shot the movie as it was made on location and on the Hollywood set, "portraits" of the actors in costume, and candid views of the filmmakers behind the scenes—all to help publicize the film. What Rosenthal does as a still photographer is typical of the profession.

Richard Avedon or Annie Liebovitz he isn't allowed to be. "The challenge in general is, they're making a movie and moving quickly, they're under a lot of pressure and don't have a lot of time to slow down to allow much still photography. The goal is to produce prints that look like the movie, even though the films used are entirely different and you can't always stand beside the movie camera.

"The relation with actors isn't always simple. This is a different form of photography from a movie, and it can permanently bare how they look. If they are acting, it can distract them if the photographer isn't doing it well. So I don't shoot in really emotional scenes, and I try to blend in—I'm one of the more discreet still photographers. I'm diminutive—five-eight—and try to use my size to my advantage.

"I also use 'sound blimps'—a padded container about the size of a lunch box that fits over the 35mm camera and hides the sound of the motor drive. You can't change your exposure once the camera is inside, so I meter in advance. I have two Nikons loaded at all times—for color and black-and-white coverage, and two more in my bag."

Rosenthal's lenses are mostly 85mm, with wide-angle for production shots. For portrait work, he favors a Hasselblad camera (a 2 1/4-inch format). His film of choice is Fuji ASA 50, whose fine grain captures rich color and sharp detail, but if light is poor, he turns to Ektachrome with an ASA as high as 1600. Ektachrome can be processed anywhere, which lets him monitor his work day to day. And at the lab he always asks for a snip test—processing of the first five frames only. This is his last chance to manipulate exposure, and he can ask for the rest of the rolls to be printed lighter or darker.

"About shooting *Lost in Yonkers*—it doesn't get any better. Martha Coolidge praised my work and the way I was working; the crew respected what I was doing; and the locations were terrific—new all the time. The Yonkers corner in Ludlow, Kentucky was wonderfully done. You were fooled about what was real, what wasn't. You assume the candy store was always there—but it was built for the film. I had to knock on the brick to know it was wood."

Zade Rosenthal's interest in photography dates from his childhood, but became serious when he was an undergraduate political science major at the University of Texas at Austin in 1970-74, and studied under Garry Winogrand, an exuberant artist with an energetic style of journalistic photography. "We got to see his work. So instead of shooting flowers, I was looking at bizarre street scenes. I learned quickly that was for me."

After graduation Rosenthal began studio photography for advertising, while pursuing his personal camera work; in 1979 he was introduced to unit still photography. He began work on *Dallas*, the television series, and recorded *Silkwood* in 1982, his first film. *Terms of Endearment* and *Places in the Heart* followed, and with *Cocoon*, shot in Florida, the photographer began working outside of Texas.

Rosenthal, who works on at least three films a year, was still photographer for *Last Action Hero* with Arnold Schwarzenegger. "It's all action in the dark," he says. "1600 ASA."

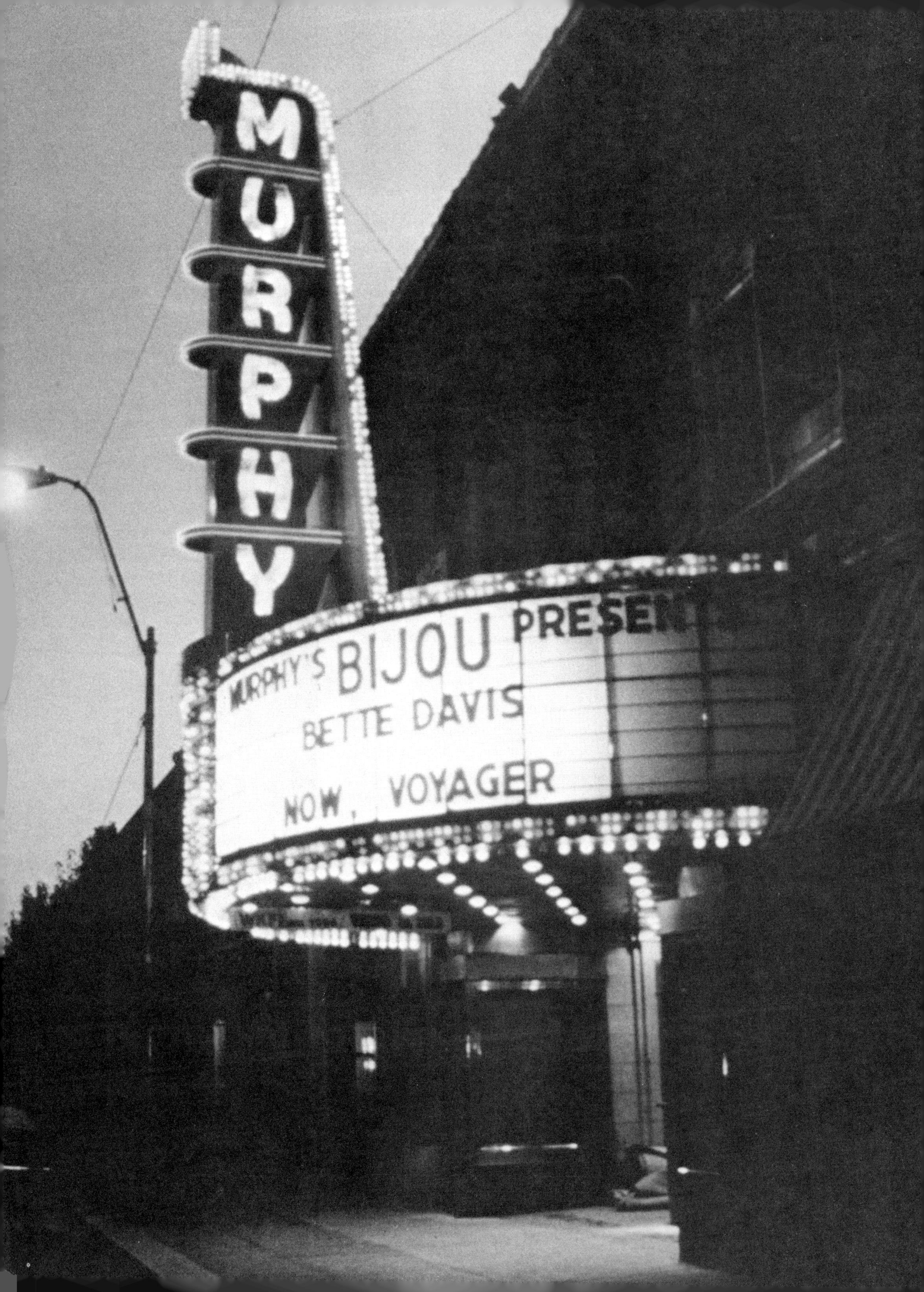
MURPHY
MURPHY'S BIJOU PRESEN
BETTE DAVIS
NOW, VOYAGER

Richard Dreyfuss   Mercedes Ruehl

NEIL SIMON'S

Lost in

YONKERS

COLUMBIA PICTURES PRESENTS

A RASTAR PRODUCTION A FILM BY MARTHA COOLIDGE RICHARD DREYFUSS MERCEDES RUEHL "NEIL SIMON'S LOST IN YONKERS" IRENE WORTH DAVID STRATHAIRN

MUSIC BY ELMER BERSTEIN CO-PRODUCED BY EMANUEL AZENBERG COSTUME DESIGNER SHELLEY KOMAROV EDITOR STEVEN COHEN, A.C.E. PRODUCTION DESIGNER DAVID CHAPMAN DIRECTOR OF PHOTOGRAPHY JOHNNY E. JENSEN

PG PARENTAL GUIDANCE SUGGESTED
SOME MATERIAL MAY NOT BE SUITABLE FOR CHILDREN

EXECUTIVE PRODUCER JOSEPH M. CARACCIOLO SCREENPLAY BY NEIL SIMON BASED ON HIS PLAY PRODUCED BY RAY STARK DIRECTED BY MARTHA COOLIDGE

COLUMBIA PICTURES

DOLBY STEREO
IN SELECTED THEATRES

SOUNDTRACK ALBUM AVAILABLE ON VARÈSE SARABANDE CASSETTES AND CD'S.   FROM RASTAR

ABOUT THE AUTHORS

NEIL SIMON

When Neil Simon's twenty-fourth play opened in New York, *The Wall Street Journal* crowed, "Broadway desperately needs a comedy, a drama, a hit. With *Lost in Yonkers*, Mr. Simon has given us all three." And he has done so for three decades, since *Come Blow Your Horn* (1961). As theater and movie audiences have laughed and wept, Simon has won dozens of Tony, Oscar and other awards.

Three Tony Awards for Best Play: *Lost in Yonkers* (1991), *The Odd Couple* (1965) and *Biloxi Blues* (1985). Best Play nominations for *Little Me* (1963), *Barefoot in the Park* (1964), *Plaza Suite* (1968), *Promises, Promises* (1969), *The Last of the Red Hot Lovers* (1970), *The Prisoner of Second Avenue* (1972), *Brighton Beach Memoirs* (1983) and *Broadway Bound* (1987).

For screenwriting, an Oscar nomination and a Writer's Guild Award for Best Screenplay Adaptation for *The Odd Couple*; additional Oscar nominations for *The Goodbye Girl*, *The Sunshine Boys* and *California Suite*; a Writer's Guild Best Screenplay Award for *The Out-of-Towners*; a Writer's Guild nomination for *Barefoot in the Park*; and a Writer's Guild Laurel Award and an American Comedy Award for Lifetime Achievement.

For his early television writing for *Sid Caesar's Comedy Hour* and *The Phil Silvers Show*, a 1967 London Evening Standard Award, Emmy nominations and the 1968 Sam S. Shubert Foundation Award.

Come Blow Your Horn, Simon's first play, was also his first film, starring Frank Sinatra, and almost all his plays have lives on screen, with or without his screenplays. *After the Fox* (1966) was his first original screenplay; he adapted *Barefoot in the Park* for Jane Fonda and Robert Redford in 1967. Simon's biggest commercial screen success came in 1968 with his adaptation of his play *The Odd Couple*, starring Jack Lemmon and Walter Matthau. It broke the existing box office record at Radio City Music Hall—set the year before by *Barefoot in the Park*.

Writing directly for the screen, Simon has presented *The Out-of-Towners*, *The Heartbreak Kid* (from a story by Bruce Jay Friedman), *Murder by Death*, *The Cheap Detective*, *Seems Like Old Times*, *Max Dugan Returns*, *The Slugger's Wife*, *The Marrying Man* and *The Goodbye Girl*. The musical version of this last film was his 1993 Broadway presentation. In 1992, Simon's play *Jake's Women* appeared on Broadway, and he wrote the television movie version of *Broadway Bound*, which aired on ABC.

MARTHA COOLIDGE

Director Martha Coolidge's last film, *Rambling Rose* (1991), starring Robert Duvall, Laura Dern and Diane Ladd, received two Academy Award nominations, for Best Actress and Best Supporting Actress. It won three Spirit Awards from the Independent Film Project West for Best Director, Best Picture and Best Supporting Actress. For her direction Coolidge garnered the prestigious Crystal Award from Women in Film and the Breakthrough Award from Women, Men & Media. Her television movie, TNT's *Crazy in Love* (1992), which starred Holly Hunter and Gena Rowlands, was honored with a Cable ACE award for Best Supporting Actress and a Golden Globe nomination for Rowlands.

(Top) **Screenwriter Neil Simon**

(Center) **Director Martha Coolidge**

(Bottom) **Producer Ray Stark**

Not a Pretty Picture, Coolidge's first feature-length film, made its debut at the Kennedy Center in Washington, D.C., in 1976, and won a Blue Ribbon Award at the American Film Festival and a Gold Ducat at Mannheim, Germany. In 1982 her career as an award-winning documentarian and versatile director of TV series and dramatic features moved from New York and Canada to Hollywood where she directed *Valley Girl* (1983), which introduced Nicolas Cage. Her films since then include *Real Genius* (1986), in which Val Kilmer appeared for the first time, and *Plain Clothes* (1988).

Coolidge is co-chair of the President's Committee and a member of the board of the Directors Guild of America. She also serves on the boards of Women in Film, the American Film Institute, and UCLA'S School of Theatre, Film and Television.

RAY STARK

With the Pulitzer Prize-winning *Lost in Yonkers*, producer Ray Stark and playwright Neil Simon continue an association that began nearly twenty years and eleven films ago. Since then, Stark has produced movie adaptions of such Simon plays as *The Goodbye Girl,* for which Richard Dreyfuss won the Oscar as Best Actor; *The Sunshine Boys*, which brought the same honor to George Burns; *California Suite*, which was an Oscar-winner for Maggie Smith; *Seems Like Old Times,* with Chevy Chase and Goldie Hawn; *The Cheap Detective*, starring Peter Falk; *Chapter Two,* with James Caan and Marsha Mason; the all-star whodunit *Murder by Death*; *The Slugger's Wife*; and *Brighton Beach Memoirs* and *Biloxi Blues*, both starring Matthew Broderick.

In 1980 Stark received the most prestigious honor given by the Academy of Motion Picture Arts and Sciences, the Irving Thalberg Memorial Award for a lifetime of achievement in film.

In his early career, after World War II, Stark was a literary agent, with a distinguished client list including Raymond Chandler, J.P. Marquand, James Gould Cozzens and Ben Hecht. Later he joined the Famous Artists Agency, where he represented Lana Turner, Ava Gardner, William Holden, Kirk Douglas and Richard Burton, among other stars.

In 1957 Stark formed Seven Arts Productions with Eliot Hyman, which he ran until 1964 when he went on leave to produce the Broadway hit, *Funny Girl*. In 1966 he formed Rastar Productions to produce the film version of this musical, for which Barbra Streisand as Fanny Brice won the Oscar as Best Actress.

Since his first independent feature in 1960, *The World of Suzie Wong*, Stark has produced such films as *The Owl and the Pussycat*, *The Way We Were* and *Funny Lady*, all three with Streisand; *The Electric Horseman* with Jane Fonda and Robert Redford; and Tennessee Williams's *Night of the Iguana* and Carson McCullers's *Reflections in a Golden Eye*, both directed by John Huston. His collaboration with Huston also includes the musical *Annie* and the boxing drama *Fat City*.

Rastar offerings of the early nineties included *Steel Magnolias* and *The Secret of My Success*; among his company's 1993 releases were *Mr. Jones* and *Barbarians at the Gate*.

ACKNOWLEDGMENTS

The editor wishes to extend warmest thanks to Ray Stark, Neil Simon, and especially Martha Coolidge for their eloquent and illuminating texts. For their contributions to the features, I am grateful to Rob Harris, unit publicist for the film, who provided extensive production notes, and to Barry Simon of Video Pak, who conducted insightful interviews with the actors and the production team.

Many thanks, too, to Don Safran of Rastar Productions and to Sid Ganis and Mark Gill of Columbia Pictures for their support in making this book possible; to Columbia's Marcy Granata for her tireless dedication to the project; and to Elliott Chang and Simone Study at Columbia in Los Angeles and to Steve Klain and Kim Griffinger in Columbia's New York office for their skillful assistance with the myriad details of the publication.

Esther Margolis, the staff of Newmarket Press, especially editor Keith Hollaman and production manager Joe Gannon, and designer Susi Oberhelman of Eric Baker Design Associates, Inc., are to be credited for both their commitment to quality and their skill at meeting unusually tight deadlines.

We gratefully acknowledge the generosity of *The Paris Review* for permission to reprint excerpts from its Winter 1992 article, "Neil Simon: The Art of Theater X."

All the production photographs reproduced here are by Zade Rosenthal, except the following:

Photos on pp. 49, 50, 55, 56, 58: Jane O'Neal

Photos on pp. 27, 145, 160: Marc Wavra

Photos on pp. 65, 112: Jean Moss

Period photographs of Yonkers on pp. 50 and 51: photographers unknown, Collection of the Hudson River Museum of Westchester, Yonkers, New York, gifts respectively of the Yonkers Camera Shop and Yonkers City Hall (photos: John Kennedy)

p. 54: Edward Hopper, *Night Shadows*, 1921, etching, Collection of the Whitney Museum of American Art, Josephine N. Hopper Bequest.

p. 55: Edward Hopper, *Summer Twilight*, 1920, etching, Collection of the Whitney Museum of American Art, Josephine N. Hopper Bequest.

p. 57: Edward Hopper, *Early Sunday Morning*, 1930, oil on canvas, Collection of the Whitney Museum of American Art, purchased with funds from Gertrude Vanderbilt Whitney.

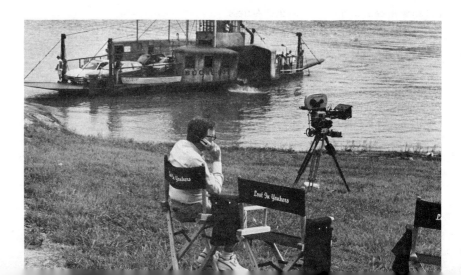

From the banks of the Ohio, the producer calls the Coast.